LEADING GOD'S WAY

Are you leading God's people God's way, or your way?

"Therefore take heed to yourselves and to all the flock, among which the Holy Spirit has made you overseers, to shepherd the church of God which He purchased with His own blood." Acts 20:28

Joseph Blessing Omosigho

LEADING GOD'S WAY
Copyright © 2014 by Joseph Blessing Omosigho
Written by Joseph Blessing Omosigho
Cover design by Joseph Blessing Omosigho
Printed in the United States of America
Published by the Ministry of Christ
ISBN: 9780979487620

Unless otherwise indicated, Bible quotations are taken from the Amplified Bible. Copyright © 1954, 1958, 1962, 1964, 1965, 1987 by The Lockman Foundation. Used by permission.

Scriptures marked NKJV are taken from the New King James Version. Copyright © 1982 by Thomas Nelson, Inc. Used by permission. All rights reserved.

Scriptures marked NLT are taken from the Holy Bible, New Living Translation, copyright © 1996. Used by permission of Tyndale House Publishers, Inc., Wheaton, Illinois 60189. All rights reserved.

Scriptures marked MSG are taken from The Message by Eugene H. Peterson, copyright © 1993, 1994, 1995, 2000, 2001, 2002. Used by permission of NavPress Publishing Group. All rights reserved.

Scripture quotations marked ESV are from The Holy Bible, English Standard Version® (ESV®), copyright © 2001 by

DEDICATION

This book is dedicated to our Lord God Almighty, our Manufacturer, King, and Jehovah, whose written Word is our life manual and constitution. It is also dedicated to all Christian Leaders worldwide who have a desire to lead God's way for God's glory. And finally to all the leaders I have been privileged to serve under directly or indirectly both in the service of God and in the secular arena.

ACKNOWLEDGMENTS

I give all the glory to the Lord Emmanuel, and I thank my family—my wife Gloria and our children, David, Samuel, Hannah, and Moses—for their love and support. I also thank everyone who assisted and supported this work one way or another. May the good Lord bless and support you all in your individual areas of need in Jesus' name.

My humble prayer is that this book will help position you for greater service as a servant leader to the glory of God, before whom you and I will one stand in awe to give account on how we helped shepherd His flocks. May you and I not be found wanting on that great day of judgment. And may we not become a castaway after laboring so hard to win, train, lead and disciple others in the service of God on the day of reward when all tears, pain and sorrow will be no more, in Jesus name. Amen.

TABLE OF CONTENTS

Introduction

My brother or sister in Christ, has God called you to serve Him and His people as a Christian leader? If your answer is yes, then this book was inspired by the Holy Spirit just for you, to help you become a better leader to humbly lead God's people God's way. You will not regret the investment made to secure this Christ-Centered leadership training material. Each chapter of this book was written with Christian leaders in mind, based on discipleship relationship, while focusing on the God chosen, Christ-Centered messenger not the message. Since God is the giver of the message, the message is not the problem; rather the problem is from you and I who are carriers of the messages, preachers or teachers of God's word.

God's word is settled forever, God's word is YES and AMEN. The problem has and will always be how we on the receiving end, receive, respond, conceive, apply and deliver the word or message from God's to His people. Jesus Christ is THE WORD OF GOD. You and I are carriers of the WORD of life to a needy, sinful and dying world. The main focus of this leadership training book is on the individual leader who wants to become like Jesus Christ in character, conduct, conversation and in leading God's people God's way.

The Holy Spirit did not bring you to this book by accident, it's for a divine purpose, to properly train and equip you to become the man or woman GOD has made and called you to be for His glory. Please my dearly beloved in Christ, be advised that it is possible for you to conquer the world, but yet be unable to conquer your own lust, greed, pride and negative habits. Bible school often prepare leaders on how to lead administratively, public relations and how to showcase gifts and talents, but this book is mainly centered on the personal life of the leader and his relationship with God, and how He leads God's people whom he is called, chosen and sent to lead by His Spirit. The fact that your approval rating is great with the world does not mean God has approved you.

True Christian leadership training is progressive in nature. When one ceases to learn, one ceases to grow in intimacy with God. When one ceases to grow in Christ, one ceases to become spiritually healthy, God-Fearing, Spirit led or Christ-centered. The Holy Spirit is the one who transforms us into the image of Christ. Your hunger and openness creates the transforming environment that the Holy Spirit needs to work within and through you. Your obedience and submission to the Holy Spirit are your greatest assets. If you are not ready to lead or serve God's people God's way, please do not go any further with this book until you are ready. But if you are ready to become a spiritually healthy, God fearing, Spirit-filled and Christ-centered leader, you must be open to learn how to effectively lead God's people God's way.

"I have been crucified with Christ [in Him I have shared His crucifixion]; it is no longer I who live, but Christ (the Messiah) lives in me; and the life I now live in the body I live by faith in (by adherence to and reliance on and complete trust in) the Son of God, Who loved me and gave Himself up for me." Galatians 2:20.

Any Christian leader who is yet to be crucified with Christ will not be able to lead God's people God's way. Proper preparation prevents poor performance, so study this leadership book prayerfully. Allow the Holy Spirit to use its contents to revolutionize and transform your life. Please note, that this leadership book is only a guide. Your personal relationship with Jesus Christ, the Holy Spirit and the word of God remain ultimate and priceless. May God bless your zeal and effort to learn how to lead His people His way, and may the Holy Spirit help you overcome anything that will cause you to lead otherwise, in Jesus name. Welcome to His presence!

Chapter 1

The Six Calls of Jesus

Bible school or theological degrees does not make anyone a God chosen leader or call anyone into ministry, God is the one who calls and chose His own leaders. Bible school training prepares us for service. While every born again child of God is called to serve one way or another in the body of Christ, not everyone is chosen to fulfill specific leadership assignments or roles in the ministry. It is for this purpose as led by the Holy Spirit I want to share with you the six calls of Jesus Christ before we dig deeper into how to lead God's people God's way.

1. **A call to salvation:** Jesus is calling everyone to salvation, deliverance from sin, self and Satan to a lifelong freedom that only God can give. God expect everyone to come to Him as they are, and He will take care of the heavy burden of sin and affliction, and provide salvation, fully paid for by the shed blood of His Son— Jesus Christ. This is the first step to knowing God. Some people come to church, but don't have any type of relationship with God. This is when spiritual concession takes place. Nicodemus believed in Jesus, came to Him, but he was not a follower until he got to the second step; becoming a sheep in God's fold.

"Come to Me, all you who labor and are heavy laden and over burdened, and I will cause you to rest. [I will ease and relieve and refresh your souls.] Now there was a certain man among the Pharisees named Nicodemus, a ruler (a leader, an authority) among the Jews, who came to Jesus at night and said to Him, Rabbi, we know and are certain that You have come from God [as] a Teacher; for no one can do these signs (these wonderworks, these miracles—and produce the proofs) that You do unless God is with him. Jesus answered him, I assure you, most solemnly I tell you, that unless a person is born again (anew, from above), he

cannot ever see (know, be acquainted with, and experience) the kingdom of God." Matthew 11:28; John 3:1-3.

People in this first stage know about God and have tasted the love of God, but are yet to develop a formal relationship with the God of love. Nicodemus knew about Jesus and came to Him. He knew the kingdom of God is real, he was invited, but he was not yet ready to become a part of Him and a member of His kingdom. Some people were born into Christian families, but they have yet to personally accept Jesus Christ into their lives as Lord and personal savior. Until they do so, they are not yet born again. If you are one of those born into Christian families and have yet to personally give your life to Jesus Christ, no matter the position you occupy in the church of God, you are still not saved.

2. **A call to become a sheep not just a church member:** This is the second step, where one actually takes the bold step to accept Jesus Christ as Lord and personal savior rather than being a mere church member. This is when spiritual birth takes place. During conception, anything can happen to the pregnancy. When a child is in the womb, the baby can only be felt but not seen except through scientific means, which in this case is the revelation of the Holy Spirit. Not every church member or those who attended miracle or evangelistic crusades make it to this point, some get miscarried, and some are born prematurely. Those that become convicted by the Holy Spirit and responded to the divine love with sincerity are those that become born again. This is when one becomes born of the Spirit, growing from becoming a mere church member into a child of God and then water baptized into Christ.

"Jesus answered, I assure you, most solemnly I tell you, unless a man is born of water and [even] the Spirit, he cannot [ever] enter the kingdom of God. What is born of [from] the flesh is flesh [of the physical is physical]; and what is born of the Spirit is spirit. But to as many as did receive and welcome Him, He gave the authority (power, privilege, right) to become the children of God, that is, to those who believe in (adhere to, trust in, and rely on) His

name—Who owe their birth neither to bloods nor to the will of the flesh [that of physical impulse] nor to the will of man [that of a natural father], but to God. [They are born of God!]"
John 3: 5-6; 1:12-13.

Jesus was not kidding. He told Nicodemus, "Except a man be born of the Spirit [spiritual birth], one **cannot** be admitted into the kingdom of God." Therefore, until you personally accept Jesus Christ into your life as your Lord and personal savior, you are not yet born again, even if all the pastors in the world were praying for or over you; you are still not born again. So, in case you are not yet saved or a backslider, please pray this simple prayer below:

"Lord Jesus, I acknowledge my sins. I am truly sorry for all my sins. I am also sorry for the life I have lived without you. I need your forgiveness. Please Lord, forgive me. I believe you are the Son of God, and that you died on the cross of Calvary for my sins. Lord, thank you for forgiving me. I accept your forgiveness. From this moment onward Lord, with all my heart, I ask you to please be my Lord and personal savior. I believe God raised you from the dead for my sake. Give me the grace to serve you with all my heart from now on, and the grace to live the rest of my life to honor you, in peace and in good health, in Jesus' name, Amen!"

3. **Come, follow me (a call to commitment):**
"As He was walking by the Sea of Galilee, He noticed two brothers, Simon who is called Peter and Andrew his brother, throwing a dragnet into the sea, for they were fishermen. And He said to them, Come after Me [as disciples—letting Me be your Guide], follow Me, and I will make you fishers of men! At once they left their nets and became His disciples [sided with His party and followed Him]. And as He was setting out on His journey, a man ran up and knelt before Him and asked Him, Teacher, [You are essentially and perfectly morally] good, what must I do to inherit eternal life [that is, [to partake of eternal salvation in the Messiah's kingdom]? And Jesus said to him, Why do you call Me [essentially and perfectly [morally] good? There is

no one essentially and perfectly [morally] good—except God alone. You know the commandments: Do not kill, do not commit adultery, do not steal, do not bear false witness, do not defraud, honor your father and mother. And he replied to Him, Teacher, I have carefully guarded and observed all these and taken care not to violate them from my boyhood. And Jesus, looking upon him, loved him, and He said to him, You lack one thing; go and sell all you have and give [the money] to the poor, and you will have treasure in heaven; and come [and] accompany Me [walking the same road that I walk]. At that saying the man's countenance fell and was gloomy, and he went away grieved and sorrowing, for he was holding great possessions."
Matthew 4:18-20; Mark 10:17-22.

4. **A call to discipleship:** Training is a must for anyone before they can master any skills. No gold will shine unless well refined. No soldier goes to battle without adequate training. It is only in the body of Christ that we have leaders leading who have never been trained to lead, and Christian soldiers fighting who knows nothing about spiritual warfare. No Christian leader should serve in leadership without going through discipleship. Applied knowledge is power, discipleship training will teach you how to be your best for God and how to help disciple others as you grow in Christ.

"Then He said to them, 'Follow Me, and I will make you fishers of men.' " Matthew 4:19. NKJV

This is where many of us have difficulty following Jesus, because we are not ready to let go and let Him be in charge of our lives. We don't want to serve or be told what to do. We claim we love Him, but still want to lead and live our lives our way. You cannot live your life your way and be able to follow God faithfully. There are a lot of believers today who go to church and have confessed Jesus Christ as their Lord and savior, but are still living for the world, not for Jesus Christ. This sect of believers serve Jesus as their savior (helper, provider and protector), but not as Lord-the One who is in charge and has the final say in their lives.

If you must lead God's people God's way, total obedience to God is required, it is not optional). God is seeking for those that will worship Him in Spirit and in truth, not those who come to church just to belong to a religious denomination.

"These people show honor to me with words [their lips], but their hearts are far from me. Their worship of me is worthless [futile; in vain]. The things [doctrines] they teach are nothing but human rules [commandments] Why do you call me, 'Lord, Lord,' but do not do what I say? I will show you what everyone is like who comes to me and hears [listens to] my words and obeys [acts on them]. That person is like a man building a house who dug deep and laid the foundation on rock. When the floods came, the water [river] tried to wash the house away [swept/burst against that house], but it could not shake it, because the house was built well. But the one who hears [listens to] my words and does not obey [act on them] is like a man who built his house on the ground without a foundation. When the floods [river] came [swept/burst against it], the house quickly fell [collapsed] and was completely destroyed." Matthew 15:8-9; Luke 6:46-54. EXB

"But the time is coming—indeed it's here now—when true worshipers will worship the Father in spirit and in truth. The Father is looking for those who will worship him that way. For God is Spirit, so those who worship him must worship in spirit and in truth." John 4:23-24 NLT

5. **Come away with Me—A call to deny self:** The most difficult task for any human being is to lay down his or her rights. This is the biggest problem sabotaging marriages and relationships today. God is calling you to take or accept responsibility in His house, to serve Him and His people, grow up to maturity and become a vessel of honor for His glory. **Most leaders can conquer Satan, but cannot conquer their own flesh.** The spirit is always willing to obey God, but the flesh always love to rebel. The devil knows how to manipulate your flesh to dance to the song of doom if you are not able to crucify your flesh daily. **If you are not**

able to overcome lust, greed and pride, it will be very difficult for you to deny self or lead God's people God's way.

"Then He said to them all, "If anyone desires to come after Me, let him deny himself, and take up his cross daily, and follow Me. And whoever does not bear his cross and come after Me cannot be My disciple." Luke 9:23; 14:27. NKJV

"[For] These are the ways of [All that is in/associated with] the world: wanting to please our sinful selves [the desire/lust of the flesh], wanting the sinful things we see [the desire/lust of the eyes], and being too proud of what we have [the pride of life/possessions]. None of these come from the Father, but all of them come from the world. The world and everything that people want in it [its desire/lust] are passing away, but the person who does what God wants [the will of God] lives [abides; remains] forever." 1 John 2:16-17. EXB

6. **A call to ministry:** Jesus had many followers, but He only called twelve of them to be His apostles. They were first disciples who served Him well and were subsequently promoted to the level of apostleship. Not only were the apostles called, Jesus called other ministers too, they were duty bound to support the apostles.

"And He went up on the mountain and called to Him those He Himself wanted. And they came to Him. Then He appointed twelve, that they might be with Him and that He might send them out to <u>preach</u>, and to have power to heal sicknesses and to cast out demons." Mark 3:13-15. NKJV

"And Christ gave gifts to people—He made some to be apostles, some to be prophets, some to go and tell the Good News, and some to have the work of caring for and teaching God's people [He himself gave apostles, prophets, evangelists, pastors/shepherds, and teachers]. Christ gave those gifts to prepare [to equip] God's holy people for the work of serving, to make the body of Christ stronger. This work must <u>continue</u> until we

are all joined together in the same faith [or all reach unity in the faith] and in the same knowledge of the Son of God. We must become like a mature person [or the perfect Man; Christ], growing until we become like Christ and have his perfection [to the measure of the stature of Christ's fullness]."
Ephesians 4:11-13. EXB

God calls and chose His leaders

"In the church at Antioch there were these prophets and teachers: Barnabas, Simeon (also called Niger [meaning "Black"]), Lucius (from the city of Cyrene [a city in North Africa]), Manaen (who had grown up with Herod [or was a close friend of Herod; or was a member of Herod's court], the ruler [tetrarch; a Roman political title), and Saul. They were all worshiping [or serving] the Lord and fasting [giving up eating for spiritual purposes]. During this time the Holy Spirit said to them, "Set apart for me Barnabas and Saul to do a special [the] work for which I have chosen [called] them." So after they fasted and prayed, they laid their hands on [a ritual of blessing and/or conferring of authority] Barnabas and Saul and sent them out."
Acts 13:1-3.

Chapter 2

Saved To Serve

"When I close the sky so that there is no rain, or command the locusts to destroy the land, or send sicknesses to my people and if my people who are called by my name become humble and pray, and look for me, and turn away from their evil ways, then I will hear them from heaven. I will forgive their sin and heal their land. Now, my eyes are open, and my ears will pay attention to the prayers prayed in this place. I have chosen this Temple, and I have made it a holy place. So I will be honored there forever. I will watch over it and think of it always. You must serve me with a pure and honest heart, just as your father David did. You must obey my laws and do everything that I commanded you. If you obey all I have commanded, and if you obey my laws and rules, then I will make you a strong king and your kingdom will be great. That is the agreement I made with David your father when I told him that Israel would always be ruled by one of his descendants."
2 Chronicles 7:13-18. ERV

Brokenness is lacking in Christendom today

As the body of Christ continues to grow in number by and large, one major problem stands out unresolved. We are beginning to have many people who belong to the physical church, but are not part of the spiritual church, which is the body of Christ. A lot of people profess to be Christians for the sake of inclusion or general acceptance, not because they want a personal intimate relationship with God. They enjoy playing church and use her for their emotional, sociological and motivational gratification, not to be drown closer to God, or for God to circumcise their hearts.

Nowadays, some people come to church to feel good or entertained, not to be transformed or changed into the image of Jesus Christ. They talk about the bible, but do not practice what the bible says. They call Jesus Lord with their lips, but their hearts are far from Him. Some people are church bound, not heaven bound, possessed with religious spirit, not the Spirit of Christ. They are noise makers, not worshippers. They only touch their Bibles on Sundays, and then place the bible back on the shelf afterwards. They only pray to God in times of trouble. They are like holy Mary and Saint Paul in the church on Sundays, but on weekdays they are like Satan in sheep's clothing. The fact is this sect of church people or leaders are yet to be broken, Satan, sin and the world still has a hold on them.

"My sacrifice [the sacrifice acceptable] to God is a broken spirit; a broken and a contrite heart [broken down with sorrow for sin and humbly and thoroughly penitent], such, O God, You will not despise. The Lord is close to those who are of a broken heart and saves such as are crushed with sorrow for sin and are humbly and thoroughly penitent." Psalm 51:17; 34:18

Why the world resents the church of God today

The mess we are experiencing in the church of God [betrayal, manipulation and deception] from the pulpit to the pew all boils down to the fact that many of us are not yet broken for the Lord. Unbroken people enjoy working and operating in the flesh. Until a man is broken for God by yielding himself to the Spirit of God, living out the fruits of the Spirit will continue to be a big struggle, and also in the area of obedient, faithfulness and humility. Those who are broken for God are dead to public opinions; obedience to God's word is not a suggestion or a negotiation process, but a divine order. Jesus Christ is in charge of their lives, both as Lord and savior, spirit, soul and body. Being broken before the Lord means surrendering everything about your life totally to His will, word and Spirit; thus serving God for who He is, not for what He can give or do. Unbroken Christians are pretenders who degrade Christ in words and in deeds. The world hates pretenders and will continue to resent Christ because of pretending Church foes and leaders, who preach but don't live or practice what they preach. We cannot conquer the world for God if we cannot conquer our own flesh, lust, greed, and pride.

Physically healthy but spiritually sick

Many of us are physically healthy or wealthy, but because of our stony hearts we are spiritually sick and weak. Without brokenness we cannot experience revival, revival will only come when our hearts begin to resent sin and cry out to God for change. When the heart is changed, relationship with God becomes enriched and healthy. The glory of God will be revealed and the power of God poured out for the healing of the nations. Unbroken people are those that are at ease in Zion, who care less about perishing souls. Unbroken people don't want to suffer for the Lord, or for righteousness sake. They hate to carry or bear the burden of the cross. There is no real success without sacrifice and no test means no testimonies will emerge. No Cross, no Crown of Glory, and No Jesus, No life!

Are you Spirit filled?

Broken people are those who are Spirit-led; those who value Christian character more than their earthly possessions or natural gifting, talents and skills. They love the Lord and are willing to die for Him no matter what. They will not trade their faith and love of God for the love of money, fame and earthly gain. Those who are broken love not their own lives even unto death. They serve God and His people with godly fear, desperate and hungry for more of God. Brokenness is not everything regarding intimacy with God, but it is surely the first, the second and the third thing that God desires most, because until we are broken the process of sanctification will be hindered. Additionally, God cannot use us until we are broken, because we are not yet battle ready or ready to fully represent Him as His ambassadors. If we are not broken, we will fail God when the winds of opposition or persecution come against us. Until you are broken, you cannot truly be on fire for God. It is impossible to be full of God's Spirit without brokenness. God is the potter and we are the clay, He breaks us, so He can shape us into the image of Jesus Christ.

"This is the word the Lord spoke to Jeremiah: 'Get up and go down to the potter's house, and I will give you my message there [make you hear my words].' So I went down to the potter's house and saw him working at the potter's wheel. He was using his hands to make a pot from clay, but something went wrong with it. So he used that clay to make another pot the way he wanted it to be. Then the Lord spoke His word to me: 'Family [House] of Israel, can't I do the same thing with you?' says the Lord. 'You are in my hands like the clay in the potter's hands." Jeremiah 18:1-6. EXB

Unstable as water

Believers who are not broken for God are unstable as flowing water in their walk with God, tossed about by every wind of doctrine, false teachings from false pastors and church leaders. God needs broken Christians today more than ever, just as He needs broken Christian leaders. God needs leaders who are not given to lust, greed or the love of the world and the pride of life. God needs leaders who are desperate for change, tired of playing church politics and spiritual gimmicks. Leaders who are not respecters of persons, wholly committed to preaching the truth and living the truth themselves. God needs radical leaders that will tell the government the truth of His word, not what they want to hear. Don't point your fingers at anyone, God is talking to you. Are you broken, have you reached that point in your life where you can confidently say like Christ said to the Father, "Not My Will, Your Will Be Done?" If you claim you are already broken for God, how is your obedient life to the word of God? Do you really love the Lord with all your heart? The proof of your love for God is your obedience to Him.

The nature of unbroken leaders

1. Unbroken leaders often end up breaking the hearts of those who give them the opportunity to lead and that of those committed into their sphere of leadership.

2. Unbroken leaders are the ones that breakaway from churches, destroy churches or cause confusion in churches. They are like breaking news that breaks the heart, because they are often

ensnared with pride, greed and selfishness. They are wolves in sheep clothing, naturally social, professionally nice and swift to win anyone's heart. They operate in the flesh dimension, wonderful outward, but unforgiving, hateful and high class pretenders on the inside or at heart.

3. Unbroken leaders are half and half in nature and life's style, they often change color, behavior and attitude like chameleons to suite their manipulative agenda. They are weak minded, weak links spiritually and could easily become converted into false leaders, who fake the anointing of God and use demonic powers and means to get ahead in the area of earthly riches and fame.

4. Judas Iscariot was an unbroken disciple, leader and apostle in Jesus' leadership team. He was not only proud, greedy, and selfish; he was a thief and a betrayer. He betrayed Jesus with a kiss. When you discover your Judas, treat him or her like Jesus treated Judas with love, patience and wisdom to minimize their damages. It is my prayer that as God turned things around for Jesus' good and our good the evil intention and motive of Judas, so God will cause everything your ministry Judas to do you to work out for your good at the end in Jesus name. Every ministry or church has its own Judas.

Every believer is called to serve

The heart of God daily seeks for servant leaders upon whom He desire to pour out His Spirit, power and grace for greater works. The church's quest and dream of revival will continue to be made vain as long as she lack good servant leaders who are powerless in themselves and are unwilling to die to self. So, would you be the servant leader God is seeking, that the world is waiting for, to manifest the power, love, grace and wisdom of God? Would you be the leader who is willing to pay the amazing sacrifice to lead the people of God forward to reach the world with the amazing love of God?

"For all creation is waiting eagerly for that future day when God will reveal who His children really are. Against its will, all creation was subjected to God's curse. But with eager hope, the

creation looks forward to the day when it will join God's children in glorious freedom from death and decay. For we know that all creation has been groaning as in the pains of childbirth right up to the present time. And we believers also groan, even though we have the Holy Spirit within us as a foretaste of future glory, for we long for our bodies to be released from sin and suffering. We, too, wait with eager hope for the day when God will give us our full rights as his adopted children, including the new bodies he has promised us." Romans 8:19-23. NLT

Saved to serve

Some of our church leaders today are yet to be broken for God; hence they live their lives in reverse. They want to be served and hate to serve, because they have become like mini-gods. Some Christians and church leaders live on past glories, how God used to use them, but now they have backslidden. Until you are crucified with Christ, you will not be fit to wear the crown of glory. Freedom in Christ does not mean freedom to sin, serve self or Satan. You and I were saved to serve God and the body of Christ. Are you serving in your local church or in the body of Christ? Are you an idle worshiper, a come and go Christian [who does nothing to help others or the work of God, just fulfilling all righteousness, unproductive or unfruitful], or you are just part of the number? Jesus saved you to serve. He wants to use you to reach others who are still not saved and to help disciple the saved. He wants to use you to strengthen the weak, uphold the strong, so they don't become weary. God need you, He needs your time, money, mouth, hands, ears, hands and feet. Most especially God want to live in your heart and show His love, power and wisdom through you, if you would let Him. If you claim to be a real Christian, how are you serving God, your way or His way?

"My brothers and sisters, God chose you to be free. But don't use your freedom as an excuse to do what pleases your sinful selves. Instead, serve each other with love." Galatians 5:13. ERV

Chapter 3

God's Chosen and God Sent Leader

"In the year that King Uzziah died, [in a vision] I saw the Lord sitting upon a throne, high and lifted up, and the skirts of His train filled the [most holy part of the] temple. Above Him stood the seraphim; each had six wings: with two [each] covered his [own] face, and with two [each] covered his feet, and with two [each] flew. And one cried to another and said, Holy, holy, holy is the Lord of hosts; the whole earth is full of His glory! And the foundations of the thresholds shook at the voice of him who cried, and the house was filled with smoke. Then said I, Woe is me! For I am undone and ruined, because I am a man of unclean lips, and I dwell in the midst of a people of unclean lips; for my eyes have seen the King, the Lord of hosts! Then flew one of the seraphim [heavenly beings] to me, having a live coal in his hand which he had taken with tongs from off the altar; and with it he touched my mouth and said, Behold, this has touched your lips; your iniquity and guilt are taken away, and your sin is completely atoned for and forgiven. Also I heard the voice of the Lord, saying, Whom shall I send? And who will go for Us? Then said I, Here am I; send me. And He said, Go and tell this people, Hear and hear continually, but understand not; and see and see continually, but do not apprehend with your mind." Isaiah 6:1-9.

The experience of the prophet Isaiah explains some major process God use to call leaders into ministry. Servant leaders who will serve Him and His people in brokenness, humility and integrity often bear the mark of Christ on them. Six things are very crucial and vital from the bible verses above.

1. Isaiah saw the Lord and knew the Lord

Some church leaders in the body of Christ today are not yet born again, nor are they yet to be crucified with Christ—purged from their dead works. Nowadays some people buy their way into leadership roles. Some people are strategically planted by the devil—properly positioned to weaken the church by introducing fleshly views, satanic doctrines, and human refined ideologies through psychological manipulation and financial influence. Some people are placed in leadership positions based on their biological or political connections, societal ties or educational status, and shamefully; personal likes and dislikes. It is not every one who calls Jesus Lord that is born again; in fact, some leaders know about God but do not have any kind of personal relationship or intimacy with Him.

"These people honor me with their words, but I am not really important to them. Their worship of me is worthless. The things they teach are only human rules." Matthew 15:8-9. ERV

2. Isaiah showed some fruits of repentance

Some church leaders are not leaders in God's eyes. Even though in the physical they are famous and powerful in men's eyes, they lack the fruits of the Spirit, the evidence of true Christian values in their conduct, words, and attitude. If you want to lead God's way, don't place people in leadership based on how long they have been members of the church, or how many people, families or friends they have brought or introduced to the church. Place people in leadership because they are called by God, because they have a good Christian testimony and good Christian character. Never place people in leadership role based on what people will say or think, or because of who may be offended or threaten to leave the church. Anyone you place in leadership must bear the mark of Christ in them, the fruits of genuine repentance, in word and deeds.

"Do those things that prove that you have turned to God and have changed the way you think and act. Don't say, 'Abraham is our ancestor.' I guarantee that God can raise up descendants for Abraham from these stones. The ax is now ready to cut the roots of

*the trees. Any tree that doesn't produce good fruit will be cut down
and thrown into a fire." Luke 3:8-9. GW*

3. God did not choose him based on his human abilities

We humans look at the outward, but God look at the heart.
God did not call Isaiah into leadership based on his specialty, how
much offerings and tithes he paid, educational status, human
connection, or his influence in the society. God made a call, and
He chose to make himself available. Nobody lobbied for him, put
in a good word for him or pressured him to make himself available
for the Lord's service. He was now saved, showed fruits of
repentance by acknowledging his sins and the willingness to make
amends. God called and He responded voluntarily, not out of
compulsion or under duress.

*"Brothers and sisters, look at what you were when God called
you. Not many of you were wise in the way the world judges
wisdom. Not many of you had great influence. Not many of you
came from important families. But God chose the foolish things of
the world to shame the wise, and He chose the weak things of the
world to shame the strong. He chose what the world thinks is
unimportant and what the world looks down on and thinks is
nothing in order to destroy what the world thinks is important.
God did this so that no one can brag in His presence."*
1 Corinthians 1:26-29. NCV

4. Isaiah had a burden

When Isaiah encountered God he did not only see himself as
unsaved or not discipled, he also saw that those around him needed
to be saved and discipled. Even though we all have the capacity to
lead, not all of us are chosen. All parents are leaders in their
homes, children lead their personal lives through the choices and
decisions they make daily as well as every adult. God is seeking
for those who can bear the burden of the Cross, who are willing to
obey and put Him first in their lives. Isaiah was not satisfied with
only his salvation, he had a burden to see others saved too. Isaiah
was willing to put to death his sinful nature so he could put on

righteousness. Thus, God's mission became his mission, to see unsaved souls saved, so they can make heaven their eternal home.

*"While we live in this body, **we have burdens**, and we groan. We do not want to be naked, but we want to be clothed with our heavenly home. Then this body that dies will be fully covered with life. This is what God made us for, and he has given us the Spirit to be a guarantee for this new life. So we always have courage. We know that while we live in this body, we are away from the Lord. We live by what we believe, not by what we can see. So I say that we have courage. We really want to be away from this body and be at home with the Lord. Our only goal is to please God whether we live here or there, because we must all stand before Christ to be judged. Each of us will receive what we should get—good or bad—for the things we did in the earthly body."*
2 Corinthians 5:4-10. NCV

5. Isaiah was chosen and was willing to serve

Many are called, but few are chosen. It is not all who are called that are automatically chosen. Many people may be willing to serve, but they are not yet broken, or ready to take on any leadership role or responsibilities. Such people may be zealous for God, but not yet refined by the flaming fire of God's word and love. Even though they may be available, until they are willing to fully submit their souls to God to be refined by the fire of the Holy Spirit, He cannot use them in holiness. It is only when one dies to the flesh that he can become truly alive in Christ. Some people may need to be pruned before they can be made ready to bear the fruit of light or righteousness. If you pray earnestly and seek the Lord with all fervency, He will show you who is ready in the church and who is not among your people to serve as the leaders of His people for now.

"And Jesus answered them, the time has come for the Son of Man to be glorified and exalted. I assure you, most solemnly I tell you, unless a grain of wheat falls into the earth and dies, it remains [just one grain; it never becomes more but lives] by itself alone. But if it dies, it produces many others and yields a rich

harvest. Anyone who loves his life loses it, but anyone who hates his life in this world will keep it to life eternal. [Whoever has no love for, no concern for, no regard for his life here on earth, but despises it, preserves his life forever and ever.]" John 12:23-25.

6. Isaiah's revelation was a crucial experience

Isaiah was already a prophet at the time he encountered God, but he was not yet a disciple. He was given a choice to either abide in God or be replaced. If he had not repented and put things right, God would have chose another person to replace him. Yes, he was already a prophet, but he was a compromiser and a backslidden prophet, operating in the flesh after the order of the king. He could not stand up for God for fear of opposition, loss of benefits or persecution. The moment he totally surrendered his soul to God, God cleansed him. He was ready to be used as a vessel of honor. That same day, he was placed above the king as the prophet of God. He was no more the king's tale bearer, but the mouthpiece of God that even the king revered and obeyed. How many unproductive, backslidden and unsaved leaders do you harbor and are yearly enduring in your local church? Any leader you appoint or ordain to lead God's people must be ready to be pruned, and anyone who is not ready must be cut off so they don't hinder others from growing by becoming a stumbling block.

"I am the true vine, and My Father is the vinedresser. Every branch in Me that does not bear fruit He takes away; and every branch that bears fruit He prunes, that it may bear more fruit. You are already clean because of the word which I have spoken to you. Abide in Me, and I in you. As the branch cannot bear fruit of itself, unless it abides in the vine, neither can you, unless you abide in Me. "I am the vine, you are the branches. He who abides in Me, and I in him, bears much fruit; for without Me you can do nothing. If anyone does not abide in Me, he is cast out as a branch and is withered; and they gather them and throw them into the fire, and they are burned. If you abide in Me, and My words abide in you, you will ask what you desire, and it shall be done for you. By this

My Father is glorified, that you bear much fruit; so you will be My disciples. For many are called, but few are chosen."
John 15: 1-8; Matthew 22:14. NKJV

God is seeking messengers not task masters

God is seeking for a willing vessel that is really willing to trust and obey Him. Someone who knows that his service to God and His church—people, is a privilege, not a right. God is not seeking for taskmasters who will place heavy burdens upon the shoulders of His people and not lift a finger. He is looking for servant leaders, messengers that will not do anything in His church without His permission, approval and timing. God is seeking for a leader who will carefully and prayerfully follow His instructions without fear, and who will execute His directives wisely. One who does not compete with fellow leaders in the things of God, or lean on his own understanding. God demands total obedience not sacrifices.

God is always at work in us and in His church. He has invited us as leaders to join Him in the bond of fellowship to lead His people, regardless of our human abilities, qualifications, material or financial status. He bids us to join Him in what He is doing and what He wants to do until the fullness of time. Thus, in essence, **God is looking for servant leaders to shepherd His flocks.** A servant leader therefore is one who leads by example; serving the one who choose and sent him to serve selflessly and honestly; wholeheartedly and faithfully, not just going through the motion. A servant leader value loyalty to God, his responsibility to God's people, without becoming the focal point or focus himself. He never forgets that he is only a messenger on a mission to deliver the message of His master wisely, yet with all accuracy and timeliness. Christian leaders, who lack the above attributes of a good servant leader or the fruits of God's Holy Spirit, may not have been refined just yet in the refining fire of God's Holy Spirit. There is no way anyone can be consumed in God's love and word, and not be able to produce the fruits of love, truth and grace, or produce the evidence of regeneration in his life, words and deeds.

"So Jesus called them together and said, "You know that the rulers in this world lord it over their people, and officials flaunt their authority over those under them. But among you it will be different. Whoever wants to be a leader among you must be your servant, and whoever wants to be first among you must be the slave of everyone else. For even the Son of Man came not to be served but to serve others and to give his life as a ransom for many." Mark 10:42- 45. NLT

Chapter 4

Leading by Example

Every leadership position has its own mountains and valleys attached to it in the form of responsibilities, vulnerabilities and challenges. People have problems, and their problems become your problems once you become their leader, especially if you are going to be an exemplary leader. Pride in leadership is a personal problem, power intoxication is a sign of immaturity, and fear of not being accepted, approved of or fear of substandard performance is self inflicted wound or work related disease. People in leadership soon become infected and embedded in the surrounding culture and political influence if they are not very careful. Sometimes internal, external or third party influences play major roles regarding what kind of leaders some people turn out to be. If you are not strong-minded and unable to purposefully stick to your defined leadership goals you can easily be manipulated, politicized or monetized to become corrupt, weak, or deceitful.

If you are not strong willed, prayerful and know how to hear from God for yourself, you may end up drawing polluted water (counsel) from the wells of fear, human wisdom and knowledge that will lead you to the path of Balaam or Jezebel. Balaam and Jezebel were leaders who started well and ended very bad, in failure and shame, trying to please men rather than fulfilling their God ordained destiny. Balaam traded his ministry for lust, greed, materialism and fame. Jezebel became power intoxicated to the extent of almost becoming Satan in the flesh, she was practically on a mission to kill and destroy anyone or anything to get what she wants. Balaam was God's man for his days until he became corrupted and was ensnared by the yoke of materialism.

"A motive in the human heart is like deep water, and a person who has understanding draws it out. Many people declare themselves loyal, but who can find someone who is really

trustworthy? A righteous person lives on the basis of his integrity. Blessed are his children after he is gone. A king who sits on his throne to judge sifts out every evil with his eyes."
Proverb 20:5-8. GW

Starting a church is easy, but leading her is hard work

To start a church is easy. However, relationship building, especially in Christendom involves a lot of hard work, patience and sacrifices. As leaders we are mandated by God to care about what is going on in the lives of those God has entrusted to us. You will have to deal with their mess, negative attitudes, offensive behavior, and resistance to change and unfaithfulness from time to time. Nowadays, people don't want to take risk for what is not theirs in this new age of fantasy. People are increasingly becoming unwilling to put their lives on the line for others, especially when there is any element of uncertainty involved. Starting is easy, it is how to finish strong and well, that is the unresolved puzzle we are all trusting God to solve.

Talking about love is easier said than done

Preaching about love is easy and very comforting, but to live out real love can be stressful, challenging and very costly. So many people today have lost the true meaning of godly love. Some have been hurt too many times, now they are very cautious and very careful when it comes to loving and being loved. Sometimes those you think are believers are those who will mercilessly stab you in the back. Sometimes people you seem to trust can let you down or turn their back on you when you need them the most. As a leader, watch out for those members who disagree with your growth proposals, some of them will do all they can to frustrate your expectations.

When tragedies happen, those you think will stand by you or with you, may be the first to throw in their towels, thus rather than relieving your already stressful job or burden as a leader or pray for you, they gossip and help spread false rumors about you. In all of this Jesus ask you to not be like them, but to be set apart as a positive example of a true godly leader. Talking about love is easier said than done, it pays to love. Don't put your trust in men; put your trust on God alone. You don't have to like everyone, Jesus commands you to love everyone. It is not easy to love those you know hate you. God is love, and love will always win. Don't just talk about love as a leader, live the God kind of love by all means possible.

Peter denied Jesus when Jesus needed him the most

"Simon Peter asked Jesus, 'Lord, where are you going?' Jesus answered, 'Where I am going you cannot follow now. But you will follow later.' Peter asked, 'Lord, why can't I follow you now? I am ready to die for you!' Jesus answered, 'Will you really give your life for me? The truth is, before the rooster crows, you will say three times that you don't know me.' Peter answered, 'All the other followers may lose their faith in you. But my faith will never be shaken.' Jesus answered, 'The truth is, tonight you will say you don't know me. You will deny me three times before the rooster crows.' But Peter answered, 'I will never say I don't know you! I will even die with you!' And all the other followers said the same thing.

While Peter was sitting outside in the yard, a servant girl came up to him. She said, 'You were with Jesus, that man from Galilee.' But Peter told everyone there that this was not true. 'I don't know what you are talking about," he said. Then he left the yard. At the gate another girl saw him and said to the people there, "this man was with Jesus of Nazareth.' Again, Peter said he was never with Jesus. He said, 'I swear to God I don't know the man!' A short time later those standing there went to Peter and said, 'We know you are one of them. It's clear from the way you talk.' Then Peter began to curse. He said, 'I swear to God, I don't know the man!' As soon as he said this, a rooster crowed. Then he remembered what Jesus had told him: 'before the rooster crows, you will say three times that you don't know me.' Then Peter went outside and cried bitterly."
John 13: 36-38; Matthew 26:33-35, 69-75. ERV

Leading can be very interesting

Leading others can be very interesting or exciting, and can be become boring too over time. When you are pressed on every side, troubled and weary mentally sometimes; stressed out by the challenges of life, combating betrayal, church politic and pretense, it may become very hard to ignore the feelings of discontentment, discouragement, insecurity and the consequences of distraction. Boredom is a silent, soft and subtle killer. It drains your anointing and prayer life until you become complacent and depressed. Don't get caught up in the web of boredom. As a leader, as God continue to bless you, and send helpers of destiny your way, soon you will begin to push most of your work on others to free yourself up for some time to rest. Using the power of delegation, you could delegate most of your task away; you must not make the mistake King David made, by not going to war when kings ought to go to war. Don't delegate your personal ministry and leadership responsibility to the Lord to others. Don't retire early, rather re-fire and rebound. People who retire early, and delegate everything away soon become sick of boredom if proper care is not taken.

Boredom can lead to sin

Boredom is not a good thing, its obsessive power often lead to sinful attractions, cravings and desires, because it creates a void in your soul that Satan is determined to fill by all means possible. A bored mind often seek ways for self-gratification, becomes hungry for affection and the obsessive passionate drive for fun type distractions and attractions, trying to quench the hunger or fill the void in his soul. If you don't want to be an example of the negative influence of boredom, learn from the mistake of King David. When he became bored, sin crept into his heart and life. When sin knocked on the door of his heart, he could not resist it. He became sin tolerant instead of rejecting and refusing it. He wanted to have a little fun, self-gratification and excitement, but he never knew that sin had crept in on him, which became a stronghold on his mind and heart. King David would not have given place to the devil if he had gone to war. Discernment is very important in delegation, know what to and what not to delegate away. If you delegate away the things that made you who you are, you are not far from fading away. David became King by wining battles, He remained a celebrated King by wining wars, when He failed to go to war, Satan crept in on him on aware.

"In the spring, when the kings normally went out to war, David sent out Joab, his servants [officers; army], and all the Israelites. They destroyed [massacred; ravaged] the Ammonites and attacked [besieged] the city of Rabbah. But David stayed in Jerusalem. One evening [afternoon] David got up from his bed [midday rest] and walked around on the roof [the flat roofs of Israelite houses were used for living space] of his palace [the king's house]. While he was on the roof, he saw a woman bathing. She was very beautiful. So David sent his servants to find out who she was. A servant answered, 'That woman is Bathsheba daughter of Eliam. She is the wife of Uriah the Hittite [Hittites were foreigners, but he joined the Israelite cause].' So David sent messengers to bring Bathsheba to him. When she came to him, he had sexual relations [lay] with her. (Now Bathsheba had purified herself from her monthly period [uncleanness].) Then she went back to her house. But Bathsheba became pregnant [conceived] and sent word to David, saying, 'I am pregnant.'

So David sent a message to Joab: 'Send Uriah the Hittite to me.' And Joab sent Uriah to David. When Uriah came to him, David asked him how Joab was, how the soldiers were, and how the war was going. Then David said to Uriah, 'Go home and rest [wash your feet; perhaps a euphemism for sex].' So Uriah left the ·palace [king's house], and the king sent a gift to him. But Uriah did not go home. Instead, he slept outside the door of the palace as all the king's officers [guard; servants] did. The officers told David, 'Uriah did not go home.' Then David said to Uriah, 'You came from a long trip. Why didn't you go home?' Uriah said to him, 'The Ark and the soldiers of Israel and Judah are staying in tents [booths; temporary shelters]. My master [lord; commander] Joab and his officers are camping out in the fields. It isn't right for me to [How can I...?] go home to eat and drink and have sexual relations [lie] with my wife [thus rendering himself ritually unclean and unable to go into the presence of the Ark!' David said to Uriah, 'Stay here today. Tomorrow I'll send you back to the battle.' So Uriah stayed in Jerusalem that day and the next.

Then David called Uriah to come to see him, so Uriah ate and drank with David. David made Uriah drunk, but he still did not go home. That evening Uriah again slept with the king's officers [guard; servants]. The next morning David wrote a letter to Joab and sent it by Uriah. In the letter David wrote, 'Put Uriah on the front lines where the fighting is worst [fiercest; hardest] and leave him there alone [then pull back/withdraw]. Let him be killed in battle [struck down and die].' Joab watched [or besieged] the city and saw where its strongest defenders [valiant men] were and put Uriah there. When the men of the city came out to fight against Joab, some of David's men were killed [fell]. And Uriah the Hittite was one of them." 2 Samuel 11:1-17. EXB

Leading by example is not easy

Leading by example is not easy; it requires lots of sacrifices and patience. It is tough job, but that was how Jesus led and implanted the spirit of servitude in the hearts and lives of the apostles of old. The superlative grace of servant leadership comes with a high calling of God and a great high price of sacrificial love, patience and endurance to pay. Jesus' motto was not, "do as I say, but not as I do." Jesus' motto was, "to always please God the Father." Leading by example is the best way to gain membership trust, genuine submission and loyalty. It is when you as a leader lead by example that you can fearlessly, selflessly and boldly be able to confidently say to those under your leadership like the apostle Paul, "imitate me, pattern your life after mine, as I imitate and pattern my life after the Lord Jesus Christ."

"Pattern yourselves after me [follow my example], as I imitate and follow Christ (the Messiah)." 1 Corinthians 11:1.

It takes dedication to lead by example

Any leader who is not living and leading by example will always have problems correcting and enforcing disciplinary actions to restore erring church members, or producing Spirit-filled disciples that will stand the test of time. Jesus Christ our Lord, even though He was and He is God Himself, being part of the trinity, followed the example of God the Father. It is very costly to lead by example. It takes an unweaving dedication, determination and passionate love and sacrifice to lead by example. Therefore, I challenge you thou minister of God by the mercies of God and by the unfailing grace of our Lord Jesus Christ to dare to be like Jesus, live and lead God's people God's way through exemplary living.

"If anyone serves Me, he must continue to follow Me [to cleave steadfastly to Me, conform wholly to My example in living and, if need be, in dying] and wherever I am, there will My servant be also. If anyone serves Me, the Father will honor him. I am able to do nothing from Myself [independently, of My own accord—but only as I am taught by God and as I get His orders]. Even as I hear, I judge [I decide as I am bidden to decide. As the voice comes to Me, so I give a decision], and My judgment is right (just, righteous), because I do not seek or consult My own will [I have no desire to do what is pleasing to Myself, My own aim, My own purpose] but only the will and pleasure of the Father Who sent Me. So Jesus answered them by saying, I assure you, most solemnly I tell you, the Son is able to do nothing of Himself (of His own accord); but He is able to do only what He sees the Father doing, for whatever the Father does is what the Son does in the same way [in His turn]. The Father dearly loves the Son and discloses to (shows) Him everything that He Himself does. And He will disclose to Him (let Him see) greater things yet than these, so that you may marvel and be full of wonder and astonishment."
John 12:26; John 5:30; John 5:19-20.

You are the Bible your members want to read

Your life as a leader is the Bible your church or department members want to read to confirm and affirm what you are preaching or teaching them. They will often compare your way of life with what you preach. If you as a leader don't lead and live by example you have given those you are leading the right to tolerate, or to promote sin. It is not easy for your members to grow above you as a leader. You preach, teach and encourage them to forgive, love and to be kind to one another, but are you forgiving, loving and kind? You encourage others to pray, to give and to overcome anger, do you pray, give, and how well are you able to overcome anger? Don't try to correct others when you know you are doing the same thing. Trust God to break and mold you, so you can become confirm to the image of Christ yourself, for then, and only then can you truly become a true example of godliness to your members.

"Don't judge others, or you will [so that you will not] be judged. You will be judged in the same way that you judge others, and the amount you give to others will be given to you [or the standard you use for others will be the standard used for you; with the measure you measure, it will be measured to you]. "Why do you notice the little piece of dust [speck; tiny splinter] in your friend's [brother's (or sister's)] eye, but you don't notice [consider] the big piece of wood [log; plank; beam] in your own eye? How can you say to your friend [brother], 'Let me take that little piece of dust [speck; splinter] out of your eye'? Look at yourself [Behold]! You still have that big piece of wood [log; plank; beam] in your own eye. You hypocrite! First, take the wood [log; plank; beam] out of your own eye. Then you will see clearly to take the dust [speck; splinter] out of your friend's [brother's] eye." Matthew 7:1-5. EXB

Make yourself an instrument of love

God want to love and shine the light of His glory on His people through you. He want to rebuke, correct and restore His people through you. But if you are caught up in the same mess as the people you are leading, God may have to work on you first before you can be fit to be a light to others for Him.

"Always be joyful [rejoice]. Pray continually [without ceasing], and give thanks whatever happens [in all circumstances; in everything]. That is what God wants [God's will] for you in Christ Jesus. Do not hold back the work of [stifle; quench; extinguish] the Holy Spirit. Do not treat ·prophecy [prophecies; occurring in the church] as if it were unimportant [with contempt]. But test everything. Keep [Hold on to] what is good, and stay away from everything that is [every form/kind of] evil. Now may God himself, the God of peace, make you holy in every way [sanctify you completely/through and through]. May your whole self—spirit, soul, and body—be kept faultless [blameless] when our Lord Jesus Christ comes."

1 Thessalonians 5:16-23. EXB

Chapter 5

Leading by Mentoring

"Iron sharpens iron; so a man sharpens the countenance of his friend [to show rage or worthy purpose]."
Proverbs 27:17.

Mentoring is a process of nurturing, training and supporting another person with a positive goal on purpose to help that person become a success or to fulfill the purpose of God.

What mentoring is not?
God created every one of us special, unique and different. It is nice and good to have someone in your life that inspires you. There is nothing wrong with learning from other leaders who are honestly serving the Lord. There is nothing wrong in harnessing or tapping from the knowledge gained by others to better yourself or to promote God's work. It is a taboo to trade your destiny to Satan through human advice or counsel by leaning on the arms of men rather than on the everlasting arms of God.

The worst thing that can happen to any Christian leader is to forsake God's leadership principles to begin implementing world acclaimed human invented principles in the house of God. Thus soonest the church—house of God will becomes a den of thieves, sin and worldliness. The day you take your focus off of Jesus Christ or make the mistake of making any human being your main focus, you will start backsliding. God place people in our lives to help us succeed, we must not idolize them, nor must we at any time allow them to have the final say in your lives. Let us now consider briefly what mentoring is not.

1. Mentoring is not enslavement
God will not share His glory with anyone. You must not allow any human being to recreate or recondition your mind with the world's system of operation. Renew your mind daily with God's word. When you start idolizing any human being by reverencing or honoring him or her above God in your life, you become a slave to him or her directly or indirectly. Slavery is not only when one is bound hand and foot by force or by coercion by a task master. Slavery is when you have no power of your own over your own will, choices and decisions. Mentoring should not have any form of enslavement. Mentoring is the needed support to free you from the slavery of the devil, human oppression, and from the yoke of failure, limitation and fear.

"Everything is permissible (allowable and lawful) for me; but not all things are helpful (good for me to do, expedient and profitable when considered with other things). Everything is lawful for me, but I will not become the slave of anything or be brought under its power." 1 Corinthians 6:12.

2. Supplanting the Holy Spirit is not mentoring
Without the Holy Spirit no leader will be able to lead, disciple or mentor God's flocks God's way. The Holy Spirit is the life blood and power house of the church. He is the power engine of our spiritual growth and development. He empowers, encourages, comforts and educate us in the way of the Lord, especially in leadership. As a godly mentor you should not take the place of the Holy Spirit in the life of those God has entrusted into your care for guidance and training. If you do, you are trying to supplant the Holy Spirit and could incur costly consequences. You must ensure that those you are mentoring, that their personal relationship with the Holy Spirit must never be compromised with their time or ties with you.

"For God has done what the Law could not do, [its power] being weakened by the flesh [the entire nature of man

without the Holy Spirit]. Sending His own Son in the guise of sinful flesh and as an offering for sin, [God] condemned sin in the flesh [subdued, overcame, deprived it of its power over all who accept that sacrifice], so that the righteous and just requirement of the Law might be fully met in us who live and move not in the ways of the flesh but in the ways of the Spirit [our lives governed not by the standards and according to the dictates of the flesh, but controlled by the Holy Spirit]. For those who are according to the flesh and are controlled by its unholy desires set their minds on and pursue those things which gratify the flesh, but those who are according to the Spirit and are controlled by the desires of the Spirit set their minds on and seek those things which gratify the [Holy] Spirit.

"Now the mind of the flesh [which is sense and reason without the Holy Spirit] is death [death that comprises all the miseries arising from sin, both here and hereafter]. But the mind of the [Holy] Spirit is life and [soul] peace [both now and forever]. [That is] because the mind of the flesh [with its carnal thoughts and purposes] is hostile to God, for it does not submit itself to God's Law; indeed it cannot. So then those who are living the life of the flesh [catering to the appetites and impulses of their carnal nature] cannot please or satisfy God, or be acceptable to Him. But you are not living the life of the flesh, you are living the life of the Spirit, if the [Holy] Spirit of God [really] dwells within you [directs and controls you]. But if anyone does not possess the [Holy] Spirit of Christ, he is none of His [he does not belong to Christ, is not truly a child of God]." Romans 8:3-9.

3. Mentoring is not mirroring

Teamwork is the road to success. Productive criticism upholds success and promotes quality. Excellence unites the team in the bond of peace. Success is good, but be very careful not to trade your eternal life pursuit or Christian values for sinful lust in a process. Don't join yourself to any evil group or organization because you desperately want to succeed. You must not mirror or conform your life after any man's life or ways. Mirror and conform your life after Jesus Christ, the author and finisher of your faith. When you look at the mirror, see yourself by faith with confidence as the person God has made you to be, who is daily becoming like Christ. Don't try to be like anyone else. Stop trying to copy what other people are doing, be yourself. God want you to be conformed into the image of Jesus Christ, not the image of your mentor. When people look at you, who do they see in your words, way of life and attitude? Is it your mentor or God?

"And all of us, as with unveiled face, [because we] continued to behold [in the Word of God] as in a mirror the glory of the Lord, are constantly being transfigured into His very own image in ever increasing splendor and from one degree of glory to another; [for this comes] from the Lord [Who is] the Spirit." 2 Corinthians 3:18.

The role of a mentor in your life as a new leader
1. Your mentor's job is to help you understand your environment or calling and how you can overcome the odds attached it.
God is a Spirit, and yet He is a person in the person of Jesus Christ. He uses humans to educate us through His spiritual gift, talents and grace for special skills. Your mentor's role is to help you stay focused on God, your life purpose, so you don't become all spiritually good and earthly useless; or earthly good and spiritually useless. For example: if God called you to be a pastor. It is your mentor's job to guide you as far as the timing, training and to give you the needed support to save you from falling, failing and fading away.

2. Your mentor will help you define your life goals
You may have the anointing and can pray heaven down, but if you don't have well-laid out defined goals, knowledge

and wisdom; you may not go far. I learned this life lesson the hard way. Goals are laid out plans, the how not to and what to do to attain the plans. It is also called strategic planning. God never said don't plan, He only said; don't plan without putting Him first. This is where a mentor's help is needed, to guide you with Bible truths and to partner with you in prayer to see to it that you don't plan your way to self-destruction. Another lesson I learned the hard way is that, if you don't plan, you just planed to fail, thus you may cage yourself in the yoke of near success syndrome. May be you are not lazy, you are very smart but yet you are not making significant progress. May be you're in business, but profitability is a struggle. May be you are a strong hard worker, but you are stranded in the circle of life. The main reason why you need a mentor is because he or she has been through that road before and overcame; now he or she may be able to guide you to success. If you are teachable, a good mentor will lead you through the way of the Cross so you can enjoy the abundant life in Christ Jesus here on earth, and later on eternal life.

3. The devil is not asleep

The devil is fully awake; he does not take a vacation. He will try to stop you from becoming the leader God has called you to be. It is your mentor's responsibility to become the hands, feet, mouth and ears of God to you.

Hands: To show you affection when you desperately need a touch of hope and encouragement, when you are up against the odds of life in leadership.

Feet: To go with you to places you are scared to dare as a leader.

Mouth: To empathize, comfort, correct and rebuke you as needed in love God—ward.

Ears: To listen, answer the life, ministry and leadership questions you might have, and of course yes, to let you vent, and listen to your complaints and whining too. You and your mentor are a team on a mandate to finding lasting solutions to your life's obstacles. In all you do, you both must put God first. Jesus Christ must be, must remain the Center Point and Bedrock of your relationship.

"My dear friends, you always obeyed what you were taught. Just as you obeyed when I was with you, it is even more important for you to obey now that I am not there. So you must continue to live in a way that gives meaning to your salvation. Do this with fear and respect for God. Yes, it is God who is working in you. He helps you want to do what pleases him, and he gives you the power to do it. Do everything without complaining or arguing so that you will be blameless and pure, children of God without any fault.

But you are living with evil people all around you, who have lost their sense of what is right. Among those people you shine like lights in a dark world, and you offer them the teaching that gives life. So I can be proud of you when Christ comes again. You will show that my work was not wasted—that I ran in the race and won. Your faith makes you give your lives as a sacrifice in serving God. Maybe I will have to offer my own life with your sacrifice. But if that happens, I will be glad, and I will share my joy with all of you. You also should be glad and share your joy with me."
Philippians 2:12-18.

Examples of mentorship in the Bible

Jesus Christ our Lord is our best example of biblical mentorship. He chose twelve ordinary people like you and I, He mentored them into kingdom pillars, except for Judas who was overcome by lust, greed and pride. So many pastors and church leaders have missed the mark of the high calling of God in their lives today because of lust, greed and pride.

"And when it was day, He called His disciples to Himself; and from them He chose twelve whom He also named apostles. Then He called His twelve disciples together and gave them power and authority over all demons, and to cure diseases. He sent them to preach the kingdom of God and to

heal the sick. Then Jesus said to them, "Follow Me, and I will make you become fishers of men."
Luke 6:13, 9:1-2 and Mark 1:17. NKJV

Bible model for mentoring

The apostle Paul mentored Brother Timothy into becoming a Bishop of bishops for God's glory. Paul poured out his life and spiritual knowledge into Timothy's life until he became a vessel of honor in God's hands. Paul took Timothy under his wings, taught him the way of the Lord, and he became his spiritual son. Biblical mentoring involves caring, nurturing the total man, spirit, soul and body until that person become solid and capable of mentoring others by God's grace—God's way.

"So you, my son, be strong (strengthened inwardly) in the grace (spiritual blessing) that is [to be found only] in Christ Jesus. And the [instructions] which you have heard from me along with many witnesses, transmit and entrust [as a deposit] to reliable and faithful men who will be competent and qualified to teach others also. Take [with me] your share of the hardships and suffering [which you are called to endure] as a good (first-class) soldier of Christ Jesus. No soldier when in service gets entangled in the enterprises of [civilian] life; his aim is to satisfy and please the one who enlisted him. And if anyone enters competitive games, he is not crowned unless he competes lawfully (fairly, according to the rules laid down). [It is] the hard-working farmer [who labors to produce] who must be the first partaker of the fruits. Think over these things I am saying [understand them and grasp their application], for the Lord will grant you full insight and understanding in everything. Constantly keep in mind Jesus Christ (the Messiah) [as] risen from the dead, [as the prophesied King] descended from David, according to the good news (the Gospel) that I preach." 2 Timothy 2:1-8.

Chapter 6

Leading through delegation

"And He called the twelve together, and gave them power and authority over all the demons and to heal diseases. And He sent them out to proclaim the kingdom of God and to perform healing. And He said to them, 'Take nothing for your journey, neither a staff, nor a bag, nor bread, nor money; and do not even have two tunics apiece. Whatever house you enter, stay there until you leave that city. And as for those who do not receive you, as you go out from that city, shake the dust off your feet as a testimony against them.' Departing, they began going throughout the villages, preaching the gospel and healing everywhere." Luke 9:1-6. NASB

Jesus Christ exemplified leadership delegation with trust and passion. He was never afraid of losing any of His disciples, or threatened by how powerful they may become. Delighted in their spiritual growth and development, He gave them power and authority to make proof of their ministries. Real success in leadership is not measured by earthly riches or wealth, but by the lives you inspire, impact and train to become the armies of God. You are a failure if you die with all the spiritual gifts, knowledge, talents and the anointing God has endowed you with if you fail to raise disciples to carry on where you stop.

Godly wisdom in delegation is priceless

The main reason why those we delegate power and authority to fail is because we don't often apply godly wisdom. It is wisdom to delegate little by little, not giving too much power or authority at a time without proving the individual first. Any novice will abuse power. Power, money and resources mismanagement are the greatest problems in any organization, or church. Jesus Christ did not empower, delegate or give authority to His disciples until they were ready. Power and authority has the capability to either make or break anyone. It is not wisdom to delegate power and authority to people based on their financial, material or educational or physical status. Be led by the Holy Spirit every step you take, prayerfully prepare to delegate power and authority. Our duty as leaders is very critical and too far dangerous for any of us to mess up, because we are in the ministry of life affairs. People [God's people] lives are basically in our hands, and we will be held accountable for every one of them. King Solomon knew the vitality of wisdom and sought it aggressively with great passion. Leaders who want to lead God's way must always ask God for the wisdom to lead His people, especially in the area of delegation of power and authority.

"I ask that you give me a heart that understands [discerns; listens], so I can rule [govern] the people in the right way and will know the difference between right and wrong [discern between good and evil]. Otherwise, it is impossible to rule this great people of yours [For who is capable of governing this great people?]."
1 Kings 3:9. EXB

Jesus' heart was with those He delegated

When Jesus sent out His delegated disciples to do ministry, He was in prayer for them, He was with them in heart and in spirit. He wanted them to succeed and was determined to stand with them all the way. When they came back with testimonies, He told them He saw Satan falling like lightning—He overcame Satan for them on His praying knees. In other words, the signs, wonders and miracles they experienced in their ministries as they went were so as a result of Jesus standing in the gap for them in prayer. He told them not to rejoice in the signs, wonders and miracles, but to rejoice that their names were written in the book of life. It is at this critical point most of us fail in leadership. We empower people, send them out alone to ministry, and we don't back them up a hundred percent until they succeed. When those you delegate fail, you have failed.

Jesus catered for His disciples and ministry at the same time; He did not separate His disciple from His mission. He prayed for His mission and backed His disciple up without compromise, so the devil will not sabotage both. A joyful leader will produce a joyful church members or disciples. An unfaithful leader will produce unfaithful church members or disciples. Jesus sown the seeds of love and He produced loving, passionate and faithful followers and disciples. Can it be done? Yes, Jesus did it, you can do it too. Dear Christian leader how is your relationship with your delegates or those you have sent out to do ministry, how concerned are you about their welfare, wellbeing, spiritual growth and development? Are you a boss who is only concerned about getting the job done and care less about the person doing the job, or you are a leader who leads with love and by example like Jesus Christ?

"After these things the Lord appointed seventy others also, and sent them two by two before His face into every city and place where He Himself was about to go. Then He said to them, "The harvest truly is great, but the laborers are few; therefore pray the Lord of the harvest to send out laborers into His harvest. Go your way; behold, I send you out as lambs among wolves. Carry neither money bag, knapsack, nor sandals; and greet no one along the road. But whatever house you enter, first say, 'Peace to this house.' And if a son of peace is there, your peace will rest on it; if not, it will return to you. And remain in the same house, eating and drinking such things as they give, for the laborer is worthy of his wages.

Do not go from house to house. Whatever city you enter, and they receive you, eat such things as are set before you. And heal the sick there, and say to them, 'The kingdom of God has come near to you.' But whatever city you enter, and they do not receive you, go out into its streets and say, 'The very dust of your city which clings to us we wipe off against you. Nevertheless know this, that the kingdom of God has come near you.' Then the seventy returned with joy, saying, "Lord, even the demons are subject to us in Your name." And He said to them, "I saw Satan fall like lightning from heaven. Behold, I give you the authority to trample on serpents and scorpions, and over all the power of the enemy, and nothing shall by any means hurt you. Nevertheless do not

rejoice in this, that the spirits are subject to you, but rather rejoice because your names are written in heaven."
Luke 10: 1-11, 17-20. NKJV

Don't be afraid to delegate
A leader who is led by the Holy Spirit should never be afraid to delegate. You must be a leader with a vision to replicate servant leaders with spiritual insight, foresight and the fear of God. You must teach the people you delegate to abide in and with Christ, not to abide in the flesh or with you. They must learn to look up to God, not up to you. They must learn to draw spiritual strength from the Living Vine (Jesus Christ) not from you.

Your job as a leader is to help them focus on God, not on worldly glories and riches. Teach them to depend on the Holy Spirit not on you. If you do a good job teaching and educating your delegates, you may have no need to fear whether they will do well, breakaway, or fail, as long as you are there to support them all the way with whatever it takes in a godly way for them to succeed.

"Where there is no word from God [vision; prophecy], people are uncontrolled [the people perish], but those who obey what they have been taught [guard the law] are happy blessed]."
Proverbs 29:18. EXB

"I am the Vine; you are the branches. Whoever lives in Me and I in him bears much (abundant) fruit. However, apart from Me [cut off from vital union with Me] you can do nothing. If a person does not dwell in Me, he is thrown out like a [broken-off] branch, and withers; such branches are gathered up and thrown into the fire, and they are burned. If you live in Me [abide vitally united to Me] and My words remain in you and continue to live in your hearts, ask whatever you will, and it shall be done for you. When you bear (produce) much fruit, My Father is honored and glorified, and you show and prove yourselves to be true followers of Mine." John 15:5-8.

God works through delegation and diversity

"Now there are distinctive varieties and distributions of endowments (gifts, extraordinary powers distinguishing certain Christians, due to the power of divine grace operating in their souls by the Holy Spirit) and they vary, but the [Holy] Spirit remains the same. And there are distinctive varieties of service and ministration, but it is the same Lord [Who is served]. And there are distinctive varieties of operation [of working to accomplish things], but it is the same God Who inspires and energizes them all in all. But to each one is given the manifestation of the [Holy] Spirit [the evidence, the spiritual illumination of the Spirit] for good and profit. To one is given in and through the [Holy] Spirit [the power to speak] a message of wisdom, and to another [the power to express] a word of knowledge and understanding according to the same [Holy] Spirit. To another [wonder-working] faith by the same [Holy] Spirit, to another the extraordinary powers of healing by the one Spirit;

To another the working of miracles, to another prophetic insight (the gift of interpreting the divine will and purpose); to another the ability to discern and distinguish between [the utterances of true] spirits [and false ones], to another various kinds of [unknown] tongues, to another the ability to interpret [such] tongues. All these [gifts, achievements, abilities] are inspired and brought to pass by one and the same [Holy] Spirit, Who apportions to each person individually [exactly] as He chooses. For just as the body is a unity and yet has many parts, and all the parts, though many, form [only] one body, so it is with Christ (the Messiah, the Anointed One). For by [means of the personal agency of] one [Holy] Spirit we were all, whether Jews or Greeks, slaves or free, baptized [and by baptism united together] into one body, and all made to drink of one [Holy] Spirit.

For the body does not consist of one limb or organ but of many. If the foot should say, Because I am not the hand, I do not belong to the body, would it be therefore not [a part] of the body? If the ear should say, Because I am not the eye, I do not belong to the body, would it be therefore not [a part] of the body? If the whole body were an eye, where [would be the sense of] hearing? If the whole body were an ear, where [would be the sense of] smell? But as it is, God has placed and arranged the limbs and organs in the body, each [particular one] of them, just as He wished and saw fit and with the best adaptation. But if [the whole] were all a single organ, where would the body be? And now there are [certainly] many limbs and organs, but a single body. And the eye is not able to say to the hand, I have no need of you, nor again the head to the feet, I have no need of you.

But instead, there is [absolute] necessity for the parts of the body that are considered the more weak. And those [parts] of the body which we consider rather ignoble are [the very parts] which we invest with additional honor, and our unseemly parts and those unsuitable for exposure are treated with seemliness (modesty and decorum), which our more presentable parts do not require. But God has so adjusted (mingled, harmonized, and subtly proportioned the parts of) the whole body, giving the greater honor and richer endowment to the inferior parts which lack [apparent importance]. So that there should be no division or discord or lack of adaptation [of the parts of the body to each other], but the members all alike should have a mutual interest in and care for one another. And if one member suffers, all the parts [share] the suffering; if one member is honored, all the members [share in] the enjoyment of it. Now you [collectively] are Christ's body and [individually] you are members of it, each part severally and distinct [each with his own place and function].

So God has appointed some in the church [for His own use]: first apostles (special messengers); second prophets (inspired preachers and expounders); third teachers; then wonder-workers; then those with ability to heal the sick; helpers; administrators; [speakers in] different (unknown) tongues. Are all apostles (special messengers)? Are all prophets (inspired interpreters of the will and purposes of God)? Are all teachers? Do all have the power of performing miracles? Do all possess extraordinary powers of healing? Do all speak with tongues? Do all interpret? But earnestly desire and zealously cultivate the greatest and best gifts and graces (the higher gifts and the choicest graces). And yet I will show you a still more excellent way [one that is better by far and the highest of them all—love]." 1 Corinthians 12: 4-31.

Chapter 7

Leadership empowerment

Leadership delegation without any corresponding power and authority to act is waste of resources, and spiritual limitation. Leadership empowerment is critical to our spiritual growth and fulfillment in Christ. It creates an atmosphere of growth for the believer to fully maximize his or her God given potential. If we are to lead God's people God's way, then we must follow Biblical standards of leadership empowerment. I encourage you to eliminate human traditions and flesh bound leadership ideals you may have learned. Submit yourself to the Holy Spirit to help you raise end time armies for God; He is our teacher and our heavenly global positioning navigation system (GPS) in God's kingdom affairs. If you want your delegated leaders to grow, give them room to grow in the fertile soil of leadership empowerment.

The body of Christ is big enough for all of us to fulfill our destinies in Christ. It is one thing to delegate, and another to empower those you delegate. Every believer is endowed with godly powers and grace, spiritual gifts and talents with which to bless the body of Christ. You may be limiting your delegated leaders' potentials if you fail to prayerfully empower and encourage them to function in their own area of calling or ministry.

"Jesus, undeterred, went right ahead and gave his charge: 'God authorized and commanded me to commission you: Go out and train everyone you meet, far and near, in this way of life, marking them by baptism in the threefold name: Father, Son, and Holy Spirit. Then instruct them in the practice of all I have commanded you. I'll be with you as you do this, day after day after day, right up to the end of the age." Matthew 28:18-20. MSG

"As each of you has received a gift (a particular spiritual talent, a gracious divine endowment), employ it for one another as

[befits] good trustees of God's many-sided grace [faithful stewards of the extremely diverse powers and gifts granted to Christians by unmerited favor]." 1 Peter 4:10.

Human resources stewardship

Stewardship is the proper management of another person's resources, work force, property or business on behalf of the owner or with the owner as part of the team. God is the maker and creator of all things. Our main task and life mandate as kingdom leaders is to reach out to people, bring them to the cross, and then point them to God, through Jesus Christ. The Holy Spirit always does a great job of convicting people of their sins, judgment and righteousness. Jesus urged His disciples to follow Him and that He was going to transform and empower them from fishing for fish into becoming fishers of men.

*"Jesus said, 'Come follow me **[be my disciples]**, and I will ·make you **[teach you how to]** fish for people **[fishers of men]**."* Matthew 4: 19. EXB

Joseph was empowered by his master in Egypt

One of the best leadership empowerment examples in the Old Testament was the relationship between Joseph and his slave master Potiphar

"And Joseph was brought down to Egypt; and Potiphar, an officer of Pharaoh, the captain and chief executioner of the [royal] guard, an Egyptian, bought him from the Ishmaelites who had brought him down there. But the Lord was with Joseph, and he [though a slave] was a successful and prosperous man; and he was in the house of his master the Egyptian. And his master saw that the Lord was with him and that the Lord made all that he did to flourish and succeed in his hand. So Joseph pleased [Potiphar] and found favor in his sight, and he served him. And [his master] made him supervisor over his house and he put all that he had in his charge. From the time that he made him supervisor in his house and over all that he had, the Lord blessed the Egyptian's

house for Joseph's sake; and the Lord's blessing was on all that he had in the house and in the field. And [Potiphar] left all that he had in Joseph's charge and paid no attention to anything he had except the food he ate. Now Joseph was an attractive person and fine-looking." Genesis 39: 1-6.

Empowerment lessons to learn from Potiphar

1. Joseph was not in any way related to Potiphar, who saw the hand of God upon Joseph and put him to good use. There are Christian leaders today who don't see the hand of God on the people God has called to work with them. God will not fail to send you your Aaron and Hur to help you succeed in the work of the ministry. What you do with them when they come to you is totally up to you. You must be careful not to operate in the flesh by turning the house of God into your family business. Only delegate and empower those God has called, we often become greedy, fearful or partial by choosing our own relatives. The apostle Paul saw the hand of God upon Timothy. He took him, mentored and empowered him. Timothy was not Paul's relative. The Redeemed Christian church of God is one of the fastest growing churches today because the church founder let God chose a replacement for him, he empowered pastor E.A Adeboye as overseer, Pastor E.A Adeboye was not his relative.

"And [Paul] went down to Derbe and also to Lystra. A disciple named Timothy was there, the son of a Jewish woman who was a believer [she had become convinced that Jesus is the Messiah and the Author of eternal salvation, and yielded obedience to Him]; but [Timothy's] father was a Greek. He [Timothy] had a good reputation among the brethren at Lystra and Iconium. Paul desired Timothy to go with him [as a missionary]; and he took him and circumcised him because of the Jews that were in those places, all of whom knew that his father was a Greek. As they went on their way from town to town, they delivered over [to the assemblies] for their observance the regulations decided upon by the apostles and elders who were at Jerusalem." Acts 16:1-4.

2. Potiphar was not afraid of competition. He knew he was the set man. Some of us Christian leaders are guilty of manipulation in the sense that, we see an upcoming leader under us as competitors. So, we begin to seek ways to silence them out of fear, envy and jealousy. You travelled and he or she was opportune to minister and did a great job. When you came back, you were given the praise report, rather than rejoice and encourage such a fellow and support him or her, you became jealous. Some of us will even begin to look for ways to quench the fire in that person for fear of competition. If Potiphar, an unbeliever was not afraid to empower Joseph, you as a Christian leader ought to be able to do better in love.

"For you are still [unspiritual, having the nature] of the flesh [under the control of ordinary impulses]. For as long as [there are] envying and jealousy and wrangling and factions among you, are you not unspiritual and of the flesh, behaving yourselves after a human standard and like mere (unchanged) men?"
1 Corinthians 3:3.

3. Potiphar trusted Joseph, and did not set up spies to monitor Joseph. Some of us Christian leaders encourage gossips, and sow seeds of discord and backbiting. Potiphar believed and entrusted Joseph with everything except for his wife and the food he ate. The apostle Paul like Potiphar entrusted Timothy with His ministry, and empowered him to serve freely in his own calling. Do you trust those under you, or do you think without you the ministry will not go on? Have you ever asked yourself, what if you fall down and die today, who will lead the ministry?

"For this very cause I sent to you Timothy, who is my beloved and trustworthy child in the Lord, who will recall to your minds my methods of proceeding and course of conduct and way of life in Christ, such as I teach everywhere in each of the churches."
1 Corinthians 4:17.

4. God saw the heart of Potiphar and blessed him. What kind of heart do you have as a Christian leader, a heart of fear, greed, strife, competition or jealousy? Potiphar was not a fearful, greedy, proud and a jealous leader. He did not micro manage Joseph or the people under his leadership.

"And He said to them, Guard yourselves and keep free from all covetousness (the immoderate desire for wealth, the greedy longing to have more); for a man's life does not consist in and is not derived from possessing overflowing abundance or that which is over and above his needs. Then He told them a parable, saying, the land of a rich man was fertile and yielded plentifully. And he considered and debated within himself, what shall I do? I have no place [in which] to gather together my harvest. And he said, I will do this: I will pull down my storehouses and build larger ones, and there I will store all my grain or produce and my goods. And I will say to my soul, Soul, you have many good things laid up, [enough] for many years. Take your ease; eat, drink, and enjoy yourself merrily. But God said to him, you fool! This very night they [the messengers of God] will demand your soul of you; and all the things that you have prepared, whose will they be?"
Luke 12:15-20.

Good stewardship is not based on numbers

The number of your church membership or leadership is not what makes you a good steward; it is how faithful you are in raising servant leaders who are leading God's people God's way. If you are faithful to disciple that one member or leader, God will entrust you with more, but if you despise the days of little beginning, you may not go very far before you crash. One good servant leader (one good family) is really all you need. God used Joseph to turn the life of Potiphar around for good.

"He that is faithful with little things is faithful with big things also. He that is not honest with little things is not honest with big things." Luke 16:10. NLV

Spiritual empowerment

If you are truly a leader who really wants to lead God's way, God will see to it that you get the leadership support you need to fulfill His calling upon your life. His Spirit will draw and attract people of like-minds to you. What you do with them and how you raise them up, and if you will empower them or not, is completely up to you. Moses, the man of God was taught to delegate. God saw the heart of Moses and told Him, Moses, pick out some people to make leaders, and I, God, will take from your Spirit and put upon them. In other words, I will anoint and empower them. The reason God empowered the seventy elders was because the burden of leadership was too much for Moses to bear alone, he needed help. It was God who placed His Spirit upon them. Therefore, any leader you have under you that is not Spirit filled is yet to be officially approved. Any leader that is not Spirit filled will lead in the flesh, because he or she can only give what he or she has. Leaders that are not Spirit filled often become burdens themselves instead of becoming burden bearers.

"God said to Moses, 'Gather together seventy men from among the leaders of Israel, men whom you know to be respected and responsible. Take them to the Tent of Meeting. I'll meet you there. I'll come down and speak with you. I'll take some of the Spirit that is on you and place it on them; they'll then be able to take some of the load of this people—you won't have to carry the whole thing alone." Numbers 11:16-17. MSG

The Apostle Paul was empowered to preach

"The congregation in Antioch was blessed with a number of prophet-preachers and teachers: Barnabas, Simon, nicknamed Niger, Lucius the Cyrenian, Manaen, an advisor to the ruler Herod, Saul. One day as they were worshiping God—they were also fasting as they waited for guidance—the Holy Spirit spoke: 'Take Barnabas and Saul and commission them for the work I have called them to do.' So they commissioned them. In that circle of intensity and obedience, of fasting and praying, they laid hands on their heads and sent them off." Acts 13: 1-3. MSG

Moses commissioned and empowered Joshua

I encourage every Christian leader to commission, ordain or empower no one suddenly. Before you ordain or empower anyone into leadership, please do what Moses the man of God did. Moses cried out to God in prayer for guidance and direction, he did not want to take chances, He wanted to lead God's people God's way for God's glory.

"Moses responded to GOD: 'Let GOD, the God of the spirits of everyone living, set a man over this community to lead them, to show the way ahead and bring them back home so GOD's community will not be like sheep without a shepherd.' GOD said to Moses, 'Take Joshua the son of Nun—the Spirit is in him!—and place your hand on him. Stand him before Eleazar the priest in front of the entire congregation and commission him with everyone watching. Pass your magisterial authority over to him so that the whole congregation of the People of Israel will listen obediently to him. He is to consult with Eleazar the priest who, using the oracle-Urim, will prayerfully advise him in the presence of GOD.

He will command the People of Israel, the entire community, in all their comings and goings.' Moses followed GOD's orders. He took Joshua and stood him before Eleazar the priest in front of the entire community. He laid his hands on him and commissioned him, following the procedures GOD had given Moses." Jesus, undeterred, went right ahead and gave his charge: "God authorized and commanded me to commission you: Go out and train everyone you meet, far and near, in this way of life, marking them by baptism in the threefold name: Father, Son, and Holy Spirit. Then instruct them in the practice of all I have commanded you. I'll be with you as you do this, day after day after day, right up to the end of the age."
Numbers 27:15-25; Matthew 28:18-20. MSG

Leadership empowerment is a must, if we are to fulfill the great commission. The church has not failed so much as in reaching the lost, as she has in the discipleship of the saved. Many people that were once called Christians now resent Christianity with passion, all because of lack of proper follow up, mentorship and biblical discipleship. Islam is growing deep and wide, and the church is declining. Some of our churches are experts in church administration, church building modification, renovation and decoration, but are novice in discipleship. We strive to maintain great stewardship of tithes and offerings, and careless about how the people make the money they are tithing on. We neglect discipleship to serve tables and gratify our lust, greed and pride. We take pride in our big facilities or campuses while we are failing in soul winning, discipleship and in holy living.

Money is not the vehicle of the gospel

We were once deceived into believing that money is the vehicle of the gospel, when in fact the Holy Spirit is the vehicle of the gospel. The deception that money is the vehicle of the gospel itself became a negative factor that lead to the backsliding of many believers and church leaders, because they became enslaved to and ensnared by the love of money. It is true that money is good, we need money to pay for church or ministry expenses, but God want your relationship first not just your money. We should never at any time place money before or above God or our salvation. So many leaders and those they lead nowadays are turning their backs on Jesus Christ at the crossroad junction of lust, greed and the pride. Money will never convict any soul of his or her sins, judgment or righteousness, the Holy Spirit does. If money was not the vehicle of the gospel for Jesus Christ our Lord, how can it be for you?

The Holy Spirit is the vehicle of the gospel

When Jesus sent out His disciples to go and preach, proclaiming the kingdom of God, He specifically told them not to take money or material goods with them, because that was not what they needed to succeed. He gave them power, the power to heal, set the captives free and to make impossibility possible. The church of God is failing today because we lack the saving, healing and the deliverance power of the Holy Spirit. The little miracles we rejoice about are the same miracles magicians and demonic agents can perform like the days of Moses the man of God in Egypt. We need God's power that can beat magicians and demonic agents hands down if we must prevail. The last move of God is going to be by demonstration of power not by oratory sweet doctrinal presentation or by strategically well drafted keynote eloquence. Jesus said; you shall receive power not money after the Holy Spirit is come upon you and you shall be my witnesses.

"But you shall receive power (ability, efficiency, and might) when the Holy Spirit has come upon you, and you shall be My witnesses in Jerusalem and all Judea and Samaria and to the ends (the very bounds) of the earth." Acts 1: 8.

*"Jesus called the twelve apostles [the Twelve] together and gave them power and authority over all [to cast out] demons and the ability to heal sicknesses [diseases]. He sent the apostles [them] out to tell about [preach; proclaim] God's kingdom and to heal the sick. He said to them, "Take nothing for your trip [journey], neither a walking stick [staff], bag [or beggar's bag], bread [food], **money**, or extra clothes [two shirts/tunics]."* Luke 9: 1-3. EXB

Chapter 8

Characteristics of a good leader (Part 1)

Leading God's people God's way is not a task any human can accomplish by power and might, it can only be done by the power of the Holy Spirit. Any leader who desire to lead God's people God's way through exemplary life of holiness must totally rely on the Holy Spirit for strength. He made the heart, and only Him can change, mend or transform it as He will, in His time and in His own way. Jesus Christ did not do any ministry work without the Holy Spirit. Please be advised that any work you do as a leader without the Holy Spirit is in the flesh. Flesh will always produce flesh. Leading in the flesh may make you rich here on earth but then guarantee you eternal doom at the end.

"To whom then will you liken Me, that I should be equal to him? says the Holy One. Lift up your eyes on high and see! Who has created these? He who brings out their host by number and calls them all by name; through the greatness of His might and because He is strong in power, not one is missing or lacks anything. Why, O Jacob, do you say, and declare, O Israel, My way and my lot are hidden from the Lord, and my right is passed over without regard from my God? No king is saved by the great size and power of his army; a mighty man is not delivered by [his] much strength.

A horse is devoid of value for victory; neither does he deliver any by his great power. Behold, the Lord's eye is upon those who fear Him [who revere and worship Him with awe], who wait for Him and hope in His mercy and loving-kindness. Then he said to me, this [addition of the bowl to the candlestick, causing it to yield a ceaseless supply of oil from the olive trees] is the word of the Lord to Zerubbabel, saying, Not by might, nor by power, but by My

Spirit [of whom the oil is a symbol], says the Lord of hosts." Isaiah 40:25-27; Psalm 33:16-18; Zechariah 4:6.

We are not like worldly leaders

God called us out of the world to be a peculiar people to Him, we cannot compare ourselves to or with worldly leaders, we are God's Levites. We belong to God, and our mission is to reach the world, to bring God's salvation to the world. As God's ministers, [priesthood and Levites] our first ministry is to minister to God, and then God will use us to minister to His people. Please, find below some of the major characteristics any good Christian leader should possess.

1. True worship: The first characteristic of a good Christian leader is to be a true worshipper. One who worship God in spirit and in truth. Our leadership role and calling is more than a title, it is life, not a career. You can retire from a career; you can never retire from being a worshipper. Whatever you do as a leader, you must seek to put God first, not the people [the people did not call you; God did]. Seek God first; His kingdom and righteousness, and everything else you need will begin to seek you.

"But a time is coming, and it is already here! Even now the true worshipers are being led by the Spirit to worship the Father according to the truth. These are the ones the Father is seeking to worship him. God is Spirit, and those who worship God must be led by the Spirit to worship him according to the truth."
John 4:23-24. CEV

"Seek first [Be concerned above all else with] God's kingdom and what God wants [his righteousness]. Then all your other needs will be met as well [these things will be given to you]. Now, Israel, this is what the Lord your God wants you to do: Respect [Fear] The Lord your God, and do what he has told you to do [walk on all his ways/paths]. Love him. Serve the Lord your God with your whole being [all your heart/mind and all your soul]."
Matthew 6: 33; Deuteronomy 10:12. EXB

2. Obedience: Total obedience to God is priceless. As a young minister growing up, God was gracious to me to allow me have some angelic visits. The angel Gabriel personally told me on my first angelic visitation that **"obedience is the key of life."** Nothing in this world pleases God more than total obedience. Even Jesus Christ obeyed. He cried out at the verge of His death and said, "not my will, your will be done." Your sacrifice and labor to God is vain if you are living in disobedience. God requires obedience in all areas of your life. God demands your financial, marital, leadership and spiritual obedience.

"But be careful to obey the teachings [commandment] and laws Moses, the Lord's servant, gave you: to love the Lord your God and ·obey his commands [walk in his paths], to ·continue to follow [hold fast to] him and serve him ·the very best you can [with all your heart and with all your soul]." Joshua 22:5. EXB

"And He Who sent Me is ever with Me; My Father has not left Me alone, for I always do what pleases Him. To what purpose is the multitude of your sacrifices to Me [unless they are the offering of the heart]? says the Lord. I have had enough of the burnt offerings of rams and the fat of fed beasts [without obedience]; and I do not delight in the blood of bulls or of lambs or of he-goats [without righteousness]." John 8: 29; Isaiah 1:11.

Obedience is the demonstration of love

Obedience is the demonstration of love and trust. Being obedient is to faithfully accomplish a task or to carry out an order without your own choice in the matter, to simply do wisely and exactly as told, within the given guidelines. Obedience to God's word and the leading of His Spirit is necessary for a proper relationship with God. Young and upcoming leaders, I urge you to obey your local church leaders only in the Lord; you must not obey them if they ask you to sin. God is not a man, He will not lie and will not spare, nor will he accept any excuses for disobedience. God will punish all disobedience regardless of whether you were following your minister's orders or not. Don't be deceived, walking by sight often leads one into costly mistakes and sin. You are responsible for your actions; God will hold you accountable for your choices and decisions.

"But the LORD said to Samuel, 'Do not consider his appearance or his height, for I have rejected him. The LORD does not look at the things man looks at. Man looks at the outward appearance, but the LORD looks at the heart. Whether it is pleasing or displeasing, we will obey the voice of the LORD our God to whom we send you that it may be well with us when we obey the voice of the LORD our God."
1 Samuel 16: 7; Jeremiah 42:6. NKJV

It is good to obey your leaders
Satan has infiltrated and crept in on some churches and had through manipulation appointed his own called, chosen and evil anointed ones as leaders. These false leaders will come to you as the leaders called and chosen by God when in fact they are wolves in sheep clothing. Therefore, you must test every spirit to see if it is of God. Always prayerfully consider every prophecy or instructions from your church leaders and ask God for guidance. Ask God to give you the spirit of discernment to save you from satanic deception. Even though it is good to obey your leader, if your leader asks you to commit sin, you must refuse. Any leader who asks you to sin against God is an anti-Christ; he or she is not from Jesus Christ and will not lead you to Him. There is nothing good in sin. Sin is Satan's greatest weapon of destruction. Through sin, Satan creeps in on us to steal, to kill and to destroy our joy, hope of glory and peace with God.

God hate eye service
God hate eye service with a passion. Eye service is when someone does things in the present of certain people to be seen, or to please men. Eye service is a high level pretense, often used to mislead people into the web of deception and wrong perception. The power of obedience in Christ is the power of life. Your

disobedience to God and to His constituted authority [when sin is not involved] will not only affect you, but could also affect your entire generation as well as your disobedience. How much you truly love God is measured by the level of your obedience to Him.

"And the Lord commanded us to do all these statutes, to [reverently] fear the Lord our God for our good always, that He might preserve us alive, as it is this day. And it will be accounted as righteousness (conformity to God's will in word, thought, and action) for us if we are watchful to do all this commandment before the Lord our God, as He has commanded us."
Deuteronomy 6:24-25

3. Wisdom: When Solomon became the King of Israel, he asked God for wisdom. Wisdom unlocks favor and attracts goodness. We need wisdom to manage and preserve good relationships. We need wisdom to resolve conflicts God's way, and to lead God's people God's way. Wisdom is the principal thing without a doubt. Wisdom can save you where money fails. Wisdom is golden, able to promote and position you for success. Godly wisdom does not manipulate, promote greed, lust and pride, rather it is humble and always seeks to glorify God. Get wisdom, there is no excuse for folly. James the apostle urges you and me to ask God for wisdom if we lack it. God has given every human a measure of wisdom. But some people by choice or by satanic influences chose to embrace folly. The serpent is wise, Satan is that old serpent, don't let him out-smart you by using the wisdom God has giving you to promote his evil agenda. Any wise counsel from the flesh will produce after its kind, fleshly impart and results. Any evil counsel you accept could lead you away from God's will and may become a trap the devil can use to catch you and cage you.

"See, I have chosen Bezalel son of Uri, the son of Hur, of the tribe of Judah, and I have filled him with the Spirit of God, with wisdom, with understanding, with knowledge and with all kinds of skills—to make artistic designs for work in gold, silver and bronze,

to cut and set stones, to work in wood, and to engage in all kinds of crafts." Exodus 31:2-5. NIV

Wisdom will protect and defend you

"Listen carefully [Bend your ear] to wisdom; set your mind on [stretch your heart to] understanding. Cry out for wisdom, and beg [shout out loud] for understanding. Search [Seek] for it like silver, and hunt [search] for it like hidden treasure. Then you will understand respect [fear; awe] for the Lord, and you will find that you know God [the knowledge of God]. Only the Lord gives wisdom; he gives [from his mouth comes] knowledge and understanding. He stores up wisdom [resourcefulness] for those who are honest [have integrity]. Like a shield he protects the innocent. He makes sure that justice is done [guards the path of justice], and he protects those who are loyal to him. Then you will understand what is honest [righteous] and fair [just] and what is the good and right thing to do [virtuous, every good course/path]. Wisdom will come into your mind [penetrate your heart], and knowledge will be pleasing [attractive] to you. Good sense [Discretion] will protect you; understanding will guard you." Proverbs 2:3-5. EXB

Chapter 9

Characteristics of a good leader (Part 2)

4. Gluttony: It is not bad to like food, but as a leader don't be a food lover, so you will not be killed with food. Be careful what you eat and where you eat. It is said by the wise that the way to a man's heart is through his stomach. If you want to easily kill a man, give him the food he loves. The devil knows what you love and your lust. The devil's agents are joining themselves into hospitality departments nowadays, so they can do more harm. If you must eat, always pray before you eat.

"For that reason we should [or let us] stop judging each other. We must make up our minds not to do anything that will make another Christian sin [place a stumbling block or obstacle before a brother or sister]. I am in the Lord Jesus, and I know [I know and am persuaded in the Lord Jesus] that there is no food that is wrong to eat [nothing impure/unclean/defiling in itself]. But if a person believes [considers; regards] something is wrong [impure; unclean; defiling], that thing is wrong [impure; unclean; defiling] for him. If you hurt your brother's or sister's faith [your brother or sister is distressed/grieved] because of something you eat, you are not really <u>following</u> the way of [no longer walking/living in] love. Do not destroy someone's faith by eating food he thinks is wrong, because Christ died for him [By your eating do not destroy that one for whom Christ died!; so trivial a matter as food must not negate the tremendous sacrifice Christ made]." Romans 14:13-15. EXB

Alcohol, drugs and cigarette consummation

Your body is the temple of God, be careful what you put into the temple of God. If you cannot consume alcohol, take illegal drugs or smoke any kind of cigarettes in the altar of God at the church before your church members on Sunday morning, don't do it in secret. When you smoke cigars, consume alcohol and use drugs, you are defying the altar of God in your heart. As a leader you should not be filled with cigarette smoke, alcoholic wine, or illegal drug, but be filled with the Holy Spirit. You must lead by example, if you really want to lead God's way.

"The kings get so drunk they get sick every day [or on the festival day; on the day]. The rulers [princes] become crazy [inflamed] with wine; they make agreements [conspire; stretch out their hands] with those who do not know the true God [mockers; scoffers]. So do not be foolish [ignorant] but learn what the Lord wants you to do [or understand the Lord's will]. Do not be drunk with wine, which will ruin you [is debauchery/reckless living], but be filled with the Spirit. You also are like living stones, so let yourselves be used to build a spiritual temple [house]—to be holy priests who offer spiritual sacrifices that are acceptable [pleasing] to God through [or because they are mediated by] Jesus Christ." Hosea 7:5; Ephesians 5:17. 1 Peter 2:5. EXB

"Do you not discern and understand that you [the whole church at Corinth] are God's temple (His sanctuary), and that God's Spirit has His permanent dwelling in you [to be at home in you, collectively as a church and also individually]? If anyone does hurt to God's temple or corrupts it [with false doctrines] or destroys it, God will do hurt to him and bring him to the corruption of death and destroy him. For the temple of God is holy (sacred to Him) and that [temple] you [the believing church and its individual believers] are." 1 Corinthians 3:16-17.

5. Manage conflict wisely: When you are faced with conflict either within your church membership, leadership or with other church leaders, always use cognitive intervention. Disagreement you cannot avoid, but you can avoid arguments. Don't fuel the disagreement by escalating it into a quarrel. Expect disagreements when you introduce changes to promote the church, people often resist change. Every change comes with a price attached it. When we disagree, it must be to probe our plans into a godly agreement, not to become a stumbling block. It is always a good thing to identify problems and then do all you can to resolve them indoors before you go public. Carefully examine rumors or assumptions directed toward you as a leader, so as not to give the devil more ammunition to use against you or the work of God in your hands.

"Brothers and sisters, if someone in your group [a person] does something wrong [or is overcome by some transgression/sin; or is discovered/caught in some transgression/sin], you who are spiritual should go to that person and gently help make him right again [restore him gently/with a gentle spirit]. But be careful, because you might [or so that you won't] be tempted to sin, too. By helping each other with your troubles [bearing each other's burdens], you truly obey [accomplish; fulfill] the law of Christ. If anyone thinks he is important [something] when he really is not, he is only fooling [deceiving; deluding] himself. Each person should judge [examine; test] his own actions [or achievements; work] and not compare himself with others. Then he can be proud for what he himself has done. Each person must be responsible for himself [will carry their own load]." Galatians 6:1-5. EXB

Be well-connected to your people and to your family

Whatever you do, say and promote must glorify God, to create a safe environment, an atmosphere of love, peace and joy. Never be unreachable or unapproachable, be connected to your people and your family. Let them feel your heart and your pain only for God's glory not to draw sympathy. Always maintain joyful mood, and maintain a good balance between your family and ministry life with positive attitude. You don't want to win the world and lose your home to Satan. Have an open door or mind policy, but don't entertain, encourage or promote gossips.

"Tend (nurture, guard, guide, and fold) the flock of God that is [your responsibility], not by coercion or constraint, but willingly; not dishonorably motivated by the advantages and profits [belonging to the office], but eagerly and cheerfully; not domineering [as arrogant, dictatorial, and overbearing persons] over those in your charge, but being examples (patterns and

models of Christian living) to the flock (the congregation). And [then] when the Chief Shepherd is revealed, you will win the conqueror's crown of glory. Likewise, you who are younger and of lesser rank, be subject to the elders (the ministers and spiritual guides of the church)—[giving them due respect and yielding to their counsel]. Clothe (apron) yourselves, all of you, with humility [as the garb of a servant, so that its covering cannot possibly be stripped from you, with freedom from pride and arrogance] toward one another. For God sets Himself against the proud (the insolent, the overbearing, the disdainful, the presumptuous, the boastful)—[and He opposes, frustrates, and defeats them], but gives grace (favor, blessing) to the humble.

Brethren, do not be children [immature] in your thinking; continue to be babes in [matters of] evil, but in your minds be mature [men]. I am able to do nothing from Myself [independently, of My own accord—but only as I am taught by God and as I get His orders]. Even as I hear, I judge [I decide as I am bidden to decide. As the voice comes to Me, so I give a decision], and My judgment is right (just, righteous), because I do not seek or consult My own will [I have no desire to do what is pleasing to Myself, My own aim, My own purpose] but only the will and pleasure of the Father Who sent Me."
1 Peter 5:2-5; 1 Corinthians 14:20; John 5:30.

Seven ways to handle conflict
1. Ask yourself, are there any hidden or unclear personal interests involve in this matter? Each individual has his or her own reason for acting in a certain way or manner.
2. Make a clear distinction between the problem, the devil and the person; is it this person speaking, acting out or it is the devil at work behind the scene? Learn to always attack the problem and its cause, not the person. You create more problems when you attack the person instead of the problem.
3. Use God's word as your standard, and tell those involved in conflict why you find it important to stick to the word of God. Prayerfully and wisely present your stand with calmness. Don't be

rude, be polite. Give no place to presumption, assumption, or the devil.

4. Avoid anger, show understanding, godly love and care. Don't cast blame until you have heard from both sides. If you must fault anyone, please do so with love, respectfully and responsibly. Don't play the accusation game at all, it will cause more harm than good. This does not mean you can't tell the truth, be wise not to turn it into argument, criticism or become judgmental.

5. Take full responsibility for your personal actions or mistakes respectfully and wisely. Seek ways to make amends and ensure it is properly fixed and encourage your membership to do the same with a goal to restore the offender not to condemn.

6. Ask for forgiveness and forgive yourself, don't play the over spirituality games when you are wrong. If you are wrong, you are wrong. Promise to make things right and don't fake it. If you do, the devil will win and the spirit of retaliation or payback will get the victory. Work to improve your relationship with the person involved, show God's love and let the past be gone.

7. Pray for one another and ask God to heal your wounds, hearts and relationship. Ask God to give you the grace to love that person more than before. Ask God to help you begin to see the positive side of the person rather than dwelling on the negatives. Give thanks to God for the love of Christ that binds you both together as one family in Christ Jesus. Finally, let what happened in church stay in church, do your best not to bring the world into it unless it is required by law. Even so, be wise and do as the Lord leads. Whatever you do, do in love for God's glory.

Hatred Stirs up trouble but love forgives

"Hatred stirs up trouble [conflict; fights], but love forgives [covers] all wrongs. Don't say, "I'll pay you back for the wrong you did." Wait for the Lord, and he will ·make things right [save you]." Proverbs 10:12; 20: 22. EXB

"Remind the believers to yield to the authority of [submit/be subject to] rulers and government leaders [authorities], to obey them, to be ready to do good [whatever is good; every good

work], to speak no evil about anyone [slander no one], to live in peace [avoid fighting], and to be gentle and polite [considerate; courteous] to all people. In the past we also were foolish. We did not obey, we were wrong [mislead; deceived], and we were slaves to many things our bodies wanted and enjoyed [various passions and pleasures]. We spent our lives doing evil and being jealous [envious]. People hated us, and we hated each other. But when the kindness and love [love of humanity] of God our Savior was shown [appeared; was revealed], he saved us because of his mercy. It was not because of good deeds we did to be right with Him [or righteous deeds we did]. He saved us through the washing that made us new people [of new-birth/regeneration and renewal] through [by] the Holy Spirit.

Forget about the wrong things people do to you, and do not try to get even [You should not seek revenge or bear a grudge against any of your people]. Love your neighbor as you love yourself I am the Lord. Finally, all of you should ·be in agreement [be like-minded; live in harmony], understanding each other [sympathetic], loving each other as family [showing brotherly love], being kind [tender; compassionate] and humble. Do not do wrong to repay a wrong, and do not insult to repay an insult [repay evil for evil or insult for insult]. But repay with a blessing, because you yourselves were called [by God] to do this so that you might receive [inherit] a blessing" Titus 3:1-5; Leviticus 19:18; 1 Peter 3:8-9. EXB

Chapter 10

Leadership counsel from the heart (Part 1)

"I [the Lord] will instruct you and teach you in the way you should go; I will counsel you with My eye upon you. A wise man is strong and is better than a strong man, and a man of knowledge increases and strengthens his power; for by wise counsel you can wage your war, and in an abundance of counselors there is victory and safety." Psalm 32:8, Proverbs 24: 4-6.

1. The church is not a family business, but a community of believers. God called you to create an army for Him. You cannot do it alone, partnering with other godly leaders in the community is very vital to your survival and success. Throughout the whole bible, leaders who succeeded did not make the church of God their family business. The church of God must be all about God not about your personal family alone. God's church must be Christ-centered not your personal family centered. The church is God's house of prayer for all people; you must not turn it into a personal business or a den of thieves.

2. God's church is not meant to be governed by rigid human rules, but by love. You cannot force people to remain in your church. Love will always win if you truly love them. Jesus' disciples were willing to die for Him because they loved Him, because He first loved them. He did not lead them by rigid human rules, but by love. Micromanaging does not encourage church growth, it kills it. Treat your members with honor and respect, and they will treat you the same. Treat the leaders serving under you with honor and they will do likewise. Don't lord it over God's flock, He is a jealous God. God loves His flocks with an wavering and uncompromising passion, He will never fail to guard His flocks jealously, especially the new converts. When you give people position and power to operate, too much control and micromanaging creates a hostile environment, fear and hypocrisy. God's flocks are not your dogs,

chickens or pets, treat and handle them with care and dignity. Whether they are rich or poor, hot or cold, strong or weak, treat them as Jesus would. God has a price tag on each of them—the blood of Jesus. Be a team player, a servant leader, not a jailor or a task master.

3. Never take people for granted. The people you mistreat today may be those you will need to help you tomorrow if you fall. Don't burn your bridges, you just might need them when you least expect. Don't build walls of limitation, anger and lack of trust; rather build bridges of hope, trust and love. Do your best to keep the relationship between you and those serving under you in good health all the time. Even though you must not take any one for granted, beware of evil association, evil association corrupts good manners. Bad friends could influence you to make bad decisions and will not suffer the consequences of your choices with you.

4. Don't trade quantity for quality. It is God who gives the increase. Any increase you get through manipulation or con games will not last. God is not moved by numbers, He cares about the heart. There is power without a doubt in numbers, but church membership numbers don't move God. Jesus had only twelve at one time, He measured in quality and those twelve helped Him turned the world into a parish for God.

5. Don't take recharging your spiritual batteries for granted. Jesus often withdrew from the people [the crowd] to have a personal time with God. Whenever He used up His power or battery, He always went back to the Father [power source] to recharge. If you don't keep on recharging yourself in the secret place of the almighty, you will soon burn out, fade out or fall prey to Satan's gimmicks or sin.

6. Don't stop learning. The day you stop learning new things or growing, you will start dying. When your mind stops learning new things, your brain starts shutting its life sensors down. Lots of information are available to our generation through the internet,

Christian books and audio/media; tap into them and use wisely and legally for God's glory. Take advantage of all the self-help resources you can find or afford. It takes knowledge to step up into your full potential; the bedrock of courage is knowledge. It takes courage to turn knowledge acquired into insight, and wisdom to turn insight into reality. Be teachable. Study to show yourself approved, make your election sure and be the very best you can be for God.

7. Never take your health for granted. You cannot do God's work on your sick bed. Negligence is the worst enemy of Christian leaders, be it in the family arena, personal life or health maintenance, spiritual commitment, human resources and financial management. You can only go as far as your health or body can take you. Exercise and keep fit. You are a soldier of Christ and must stay constantly fit to be ready for battle at all times. Take some time to laugh; laughter is medicine to the soul. Don't be all ministry good and be socially useless. Make room to spend some good quality laughing time with your family. If you are not married or don't have children yet, enjoy some godly healthy fun type bible games with your church members or other church leaders. Take good care of your body, if you want to live long, God will not do it for you. Health is wealth, do all you can to treasure your health more than gold.

8. Don't let success get into your head. If you do, you can gain the world and may lose your soul. Success principles, skills and hard work can get you to the top, but you need God's grace to stay on top. Real success is helping others succeed. Obstacles are a necessary factor to success; victory can be obtained after many struggles and failures. Success is not how much you were able to acquire or waste in lustful or prideful living, but what you did to help God's His people become what He created them to be. Don't allow success and fame to draw you away from God, or for success to become a snare in your relationship with God instead of being a blessing.

9. Don't take confidentiality for granted. Properly safeguard your people's confidential information. If you betray your people (church members) trust and confidence, you have betrayed your trust, love, and respect. The devil is waiting and hoping you will fall or fail, give him no place to come in, to steal, kill and destroy you.

"Everything that goes into a life of pleasing God has been miraculously given to us by getting to know, personally and intimately, the One who invited us to God. The best invitation we ever received! We were also given absolutely terrific promises to pass on to you—your tickets to participation in the life of God after you turned your back on a world corrupted by lust. So don't lose a minute in building on what you've been given, complementing your basic faith with good character, spiritual understanding, alert discipline, passionate patience, reverent wonder, warm friendliness, and generous love, each dimension fitting into and developing the others. With these qualities active and growing in your lives, no grass will grow under your feet, no day will pass without its reward as you mature in your experience of our Master Jesus. Without these qualities you can't see what's right before you, oblivious that your old sinful life has been wiped off the books." 2 Peter 1: 3-7. MSG

Chapter 11

Leadership counsel from the heart (Part 2)

1. Don't let pride destroy you: Pride is a snare and a destroyer. Pride blinds and creates false glory. Pride kills. God resist the proud, but give grace to the humble. If you are to lead God's people God's way, pride must be completely rooted out of your life. Don't be proud, be humble. Jesus Christ remained humbled to the end, even up to His death on the Cross.

"Pride [Insolence] leads only to shame; it is wise to be humble. The Lord will tear down [uproot] the proud person's house, but he will protect [establish] the widow's property [boundaries]. A greedy person causes trouble [stirs up conflict], but the one who trusts the Lord will succeed [escape]." Proverbs 11:2; 15: 25; 28: 25. EXB

"Your pride can bring you down. Humility will bring you honor. Edom, you made other nations afraid, so you thought you were important. But your pride has fooled you. You live in caves, high on the cliff. Your home is high in the hills. But even if you build your home as high as an eagle's nest, I will bring you down from there." This is what the Lord said. Listen and pay attention. The Lord has spoken to you. Do not be proud." Proverbs 29: 23; Jeremiah 49: 16; 13: 15. ERV

2. Don't love money. The love of money corrupts God's love, good manners and good judgment. Money itself is not bad; you and I need money to enjoy a better life. What is bad about the love of money is how some of us become negatively influenced (caged) by the power of its love, spirit of greed; that we slow but surely begin to neglect God's way (Word) to satisfy the lust of the flesh and of the eyes. Certainly, the love of money is the root of all kinds of evil, lies, lust, greed and pride. Some devoted and powerful Christian leaders who set their hearts to love money, and embarked

on getting rich by all means possible, have wandered away from the high way of holiness. "No one can serve two masters, either he will hate the one or love the other." You cannot serve GOD and MONEY. Those who love money often indulge themselves in all kinds of sinful ways, trying to fill the void in their soul. Keep your life free from the love of money and be content. Money lovers glory in the flesh (perishable) things, not in Christ—our hope of glory.

The Love of money can be deadly

The Love of money is deadly. Monetary gain, material gain, lust and pride are Satan's greatest weapons against church leaders nowadays. If you have fallen into the bondage of the love of money, return to God now while you may.

"An elder must be such a good man that no one can rightly criticize him. He must be faithful to his wife. He must have self-control and be wise. He must be respected by others. He must be ready to help people by welcoming them into his home. He must be a good teacher. He must not drink too much, and he must not be someone who likes to fight. He must be gentle and peaceful. He must not be someone who loves money. He must be a good leader of his own family. This means that his children obey him with full respect. If a man does not know how to lead his own family, he will not be able to take care of God's church. An elder must not be a new believer. It might make him too proud of himself. Then he would be condemned for his pride the same as the devil was. An elder must also have the respect of people who are not part of the church. Then he will not be criticized by others and be caught in the devil's trap.

In the same way, the men who are chosen to be special servants must have the respect of others. They must not be men who say things they don't mean or who spend their time drinking too much. They must not be men who will do almost anything for money. They must follow the true faith that God has now made known to us and always do what they know is right. You

should <u>test</u> them first. Then, if you find that they have done nothing wrong, they can be special servants. In the same way, the women must have the respect of others. They must not be women who speak evil about other people. They must have self-control and be women who can be trusted in everything. The men who are special servants must be faithful in marriage. They must be good leaders of children and their own families."
1 Timothy 3: 2-12. ERV

3. Don't quit when things are hard. Impatience was once my major problem in the ministry; I did not have any endurance at a time. When things got tough and hard, I backed off and lean on other available alternatives. This was my nature and behavior for a long time until God told me, I would not go far, but continued to run around in the circle of un-fulfillment. I had to learn how to persevere the hard way; I believed now that God allowed me to go through, so you don't have to. Perseverance is when you are making little or no progress, but refusing to be distracted or quit, pursuing the vision or goals set before you by faith that God will not fail. To persevere is to be persistence, continuing to endure with an unwavering faith with patience, staying the course against all odds, difficulties, obstacles and discouragement. Stay focused on God's will, keep to your original calling, don't be here and there, be yourself and fulfill your destiny. Anchor your faith to Jesus Christ our firm foundation. He will not let you down.

The devil is not really after you as a godly leader, he is out to get to God's people through you. So he can use you as a channel to steal, kill and destroy them. Sometimes things will be hard. Trials will come, life's wind will blow against you; don't give up. As a good soldier of Christ you must learn to endure hardness. No matter the situation you are in, the situation must not control you. You must not give in, or give up your hope in the shore of failure; failing is not the end of life. Failures are success lessons learn the hard way and turned inside out to inspiring testimonies of God's faithfulness. Whenever you feel down or discouraged, go back to God, the source of life and find out where you midst it. If you still need some encouragement to boost you up after that, please search and get our book titled: "Knocked Down, But Not Knocked Out." It will not only help you regain hope and courage, it will also help place you back in the arena of life to win. The apostle Paul was a man of like passion as you and me, through faith and perseverance he was able to overcome against all odds to finish well and strong.

Stop complaining, persevere

"Don't blame the circumstances around you or what you have become on others, circumstances don't makes decisions, you do. Take responsibility and go forward with resilience. God never promised us a troubled free life, He promised us that the trails of our faith will produces patience, if we are able to wait and lean on Him, not on our own understanding. As for falling, every one of us has fallen before and may fall again. Only fools stay down when they fall. Testimonies are given birth to through trials. If you don't want test and trials, you may not have testimonies. Fear is the number one enemy of faith and the number two enemy of perseverance and hope. Until you are able to conquer your fear, you will continue to be slave to it. "Faith and courage are the greatest enemies of fear, faith is the power of courage, but the only courage there is and will ever be is that which is driven by perseverance." Stop complaining and stop nursing your fear. Persevere, do something good with your life, you only have one life to live!

"Be careful [conscientious] in your life [about yourself] and in your teaching. If you continue to live and teach rightly [persevere in these things], you will save both yourself and those who listen to you. When people are tempted and still continue strong, they should be happy [Blessed is the one who perseveres/endures trials/temptations]. After they have proved their faith [stood/endured/passed the test], God will reward them with life forever [they will receive the crown of life; alludes to the laurel crown given for a victory]. God [He] promised this to all those who love him. So do not lose [throw away] ·the courage you had in the past [or your confident trust in God; or your boldness],

which has a great <u>reward</u>. You must hold on [persevere; endure], so you can do what God wants [the will of God] and receive what he has promised."
1 Timothy 4: 16; James 1: 12; Hebrews 10: 35-36. EXB

Don't allow anything or anyone to corrupt your love for God
I don't know about you, what keeps me going forward and upward in ministry against all odds is the love I have for Jesus Christ, the One who loved me and gave His life a ransom for me. No greater love than the love of Jesus Christ my Lord, nothing in this world can separate me from the love of Jesus Christ.

"Love never gives up, never loses faith, is always hopeful, and endures through every circumstance. Prophecy and speaking in unknown languages and special knowledge will become useless. But love will last forever! Now our knowledge is partial and <u>incomplete</u>, and even the gift of prophecy reveals only part of the whole picture! But when the time of perfection comes, these partial things will become useless. When I was a child, I spoke and thought and reasoned as a child. But when I grew up, I put away childish things. <u>Now</u> we see things imperfectly, like puzzling reflections in a mirror, but then we will see everything with perfect clarity. All that I know now is partial and incomplete, but then I will know everything completely, just as God now knows me completely. Three things will last forever—faith, hope, and love— and the greatest of these is love. But you are not controlled by your sinful nature.

You are controlled by the Spirit if you have the Spirit of God living in you. (And remember that those who do not have the Spirit of Christ living in them do not belong to him at all.) And Christ lives within you, so even though your body will die because of sin, the Spirit gives you life because you have been made right with God. The Spirit of God, who raised Jesus from the dead, lives in you. And just as God raised Christ Jesus from the dead, he will give life to your mortal bodies by this same Spirit living within you. Therefore, dear brothers and sisters, you have no obligation to do *what your sinful nature urges you to do. For if you live by its dictates, you will die. But if through the <u>power</u> of the Spirit you put to death the deeds of your sinful nature, you will live. For all who are led by the Spirit of God are children of God. So you have not received a spirit that makes you fearful slaves.*

Instead, you received God's Spirit when he adopted you as his own children. <u>Now</u> we call him, "Abba, Father." For his Spirit joins with our spirit to affirm that we are God's children. And since we are his children, we are his heirs. In fact, together with Christ we are heirs of God's glory. But if we are to share his glory, we must also share his suffering. Yet what we suffer now is nothing compared to the glory he will reveal to us later. For all creation is waiting eagerly for that future day when God will reveal who his children really are. Against its will, all creation was subjected to God's curse. But with eager hope, the creation looks forward to the day when it will <u>join</u> God's children in glorious freedom from death and decay." 1 Corinthians 13: 7-13; Romans 8: 9-21. NLT

Chapter 12

Leadership counsel from the heart (Part 3)

1. Don't take appreciation for granted. Appreciate those serving under you; acknowledge their good work and labor of love. Show gratitude and recognize their sacrifices. Give rewards when you can, nothing is too big or too small to be thankful for. The less you appreciate people, the more your congregation depreciates. The more you sincerely appreciate the people God has placed in your life, the more the joy and commitment, dedication and sacrificial love you will attract. Appreciating more consistently offer many blessings and promotes teamwork. Appreciation activates love, creates enthusiasm and propels perseverance. Developing a good attitude of appreciation may become your greatest asset in time of need. People don't easily forget how you treat them.

"It is a proof of your faith. Many people will praise [glorify] God because you obey [submit to] the Good News [Gospel] of Christ—the gospel you say you believe [confess]—and because you freely [generously] share with them and with all others. And when they pray for you, they will wish they could be with [long for] you because of the great grace that God has given you.
Thanks be to God for his ·gift that is too wonderful for words [indescribable/inexpressible gift]. First I want to say that I thank my God through Jesus Christ for all of you, because people everywhere in the world are talking about your faith. God, whom I serve with my whole heart [in/with my spirit] by telling [or for the sake of; in] the Good News [Gospel] about his Son, knows [is my witness] that I always [continually; never cease to] mention you every time I pray. I pray that now at last if God wants it [by God's will] I will be allowed to come [succeed in coming] to you. I want very much [long] to see you, to give [impart to; or share with] you some spiritual gift to make you strong. I mean that I want us to help each other [be mutually encouraged/comforted] with the faith

we have [by each other's faith]. Your faith will help me, and my faith will help you [both yours and mine]."
2 Corinthians 9:13-15; Romans 1: 8-12. EXB

2. Don't neglect the power of networking. A good leader must be a resourceful networker, able to connect and bring the right people together to get things done. The power of positive networking remains the greatest marketing tool in the world today. Proper networking is a vital tool for us to use in winning the world for God. Networking is the gateway to growth and advancement. Networking will help you as a leader launch into new successful heights beyond your widest dream.

God is a good networker
There are different kinds of networking, business; career, leadership, membership and Christian networking just to name a few. Networking is for mutual or spiritual gain, while promoting diversity. Church growth relies heavily upon effective networking to reach people you will ordinarily not be able to reach for Christ. Networking is simply becoming part of a winning team, doing life together, sharing resources, good information and spiritual truths. God is a networker. He is able to bring people together from all walks of life under one roof—the body of Christ. Your ability as a Spirit filled leader to network must be very good. You must understand that when God called you into leadership, He also called you to be a marketer and a networker in His soul saving mission as His ambassador. Train your leadership team and equipped them to market God's kingdom visas. To be a good networker, you must be diligent, be open to positive ideals and wise counsel. Don't be narrow-minded. When people give you good godly ideas and information, receive it with open heart and be grateful.

A good networker is an investor
A good networker is an investor. If you can get one person to commit, invest in discipleship, use that one person to reach others. Therefore, any opportunity God gives you, use it to sow the seeds

of love. Good networking require prayers and the leading of the Spirit of God. Remember, it is not about you but about Jesus and Him alone. To be a good networker, you must be a good listener and a person of character. Conduct your networking prayerfully and wisely. Lead by example, invest in marketing. The apostle Paul was a good networker.

"I am free and belong to no one. But I make myself a slave to all people to win as many as I can. To the Jews I became like a Jew to win the Jews. I myself am not ruled by [subject to; under] the law. But to those who are ruled by [subject to; under] the law I became like a person who is ruled by [subject to; under] the law. I did this to win those who are ruled by [subject to; under] the law. To those who are without the law [Gentiles] I became like a person who is without the law. I did this to win those people who are without the law. (But really, I am not without God's law—I am ruled by [under] Christ's law.)

To those who are weak [in faith], I became weak so I could win the weak. I have become all things to all people so I could save some of them in any way possible. I do all this because of the Good News [Gospel] and so I can share in its blessings [or be a participant in it]. You [Don't you...?] know that in a race [stadium] all the runners run, but only one gets the prize. So run to win! All those who compete in the games use self-control [train with strict discipline] so they can win a crown [victor's wreath]. That crown [victor's wreath] is an earthly thing that lasts only a short time [perishable], but our crown will never be destroyed [is imperishable]. So I do not run without a goal [aimlessly]. I fight like a boxer who is hitting something—not just the air." 1 Corinthians 9: 19-26. EXB

3. Don't neglect the power of Prayer. Prayer is your warfare bomber machinery. There is no doubt in my mind that the time we are living in is injury time. Satan is all out and ready to pour out his worst fury, or to release his ballistic missiles against us. God is looking and seeking for selfless, fearless and single hearted men

and women He can use to withstand the Goliaths of our time. God is seeking for a leader who is ready, willing and prepared to sacrifice his or her Isaac for Him. A leader who is ready to die to self (lust), pride and greed. God is looking for leaders to incubate in the womb of prayer, filled with uncompromising passion for lost souls, holiness, and the power for the revival we desperate need today.

No prayer, no life

A prayerful leader is a warrior not a mere man. It is at the altar of prayer that God distributes the keys of the kingdom—to destroy satanic strongholds and free the children of men from satanic prisons. The greatest gift any leader can give to his ministry leaders or church members is the gift of sincere, earnest and fervent prayer. Prayer brings life, sustains life and establishes life with evergreen leaves on the sea shore of God's faithfulness. If there is no prayer there is no life. For that which is born of the Spirit is Spirit. Our own power and might will get us nowhere, because, we cannot win spiritual wars with carnal weapons. Money, materialism and fame are not welcome in the holy of holies. Educational status and oratory presentation skills cannot bind demons. The total sum of all fleshly fights and labor is this: "for by flesh shall no man prevail." Prayer works because God is always at work, and prayer will not fail because God fails not. We will not see the supernatural move of God in our days unless we pray. God can use an ordinary man to accomplish extraordinary things through the power of prayer. Prayer changes things and nothing is impossible to those who believe in the power of prayer. No prayer, no abundant life.

*"Be anxious for nothing, but **in everything by prayer** and **supplication,** with thanksgiving, let your requests be made known to God; and the peace of God, which surpasses all understanding, will guard your hearts and minds through Christ Jesus."* Philippians 4:6-7. NKJV

4. Don't set your heart and life passion on spiritual gifts, seek the fruits of the Spirit. All spiritual gifts will all end here on earth. What will guarantee you eternal life are the fruits of the Spirit. Stop laboring for the things that will one day cease and start laboring for the things that will last forever. Ask God to give you the grace to develop good leadership qualities—the fruits of His Holy Spirit. The fruits of the Spirit are resident in every believer, but they are often inactive until you and I activate them through total submission, obedience to God and self determination to crucify the flesh. Believe it or not, it is very possible to heal the sick, raise the dead, cast and demons, be financially free here on earth and at the end go to hell. On the other hand, it is impossible to possess the fruits of the spirit and not go to heaven.

"But the Spirit produces the fruit of [fruit of the Spirit is] love, joy, peace, patience, kindness, goodness, faithfulness [or faith], gentleness, self-control. There is no law that says these things are wrong [or No law can oppose such things]. Those who belong to Christ Jesus have crucified ·their own sinful selves [the sinful nature; the flesh]. They have given up their old selfish feelings and the evil things they wanted to do [its passions and desires].

We [If/Since we…] get our new life from the Spirit [live by the Spirit], so we should follow [be guided by; walk in step with] the Spirit. Because you have these blessings [For this very reason; the reasons stated in], do your best [make every effort; strive] to add these things to [or increase these things in] your lives: to your faith, add goodness [virtue; moral excellence]; and to your goodness [virtue; moral excellence], add knowledge; and to your knowledge, add self-control; and to your self-control, add patience [or perseverance]; and to your patience [or perseverance], add service for God [devotion; piety; godliness]; and to your service for God [devotion; piety; godliness], add kindness for your brothers and sisters in Christ [affection for fellow believers; brotherly love/affection]; and to this kindness [affection; brotherly love/affection], add love [Greek: agape]. If all these things are in you and are growing [increasing], they will help you to be useful

and productive [keep you from being ineffective/idle and unfruitful/unproductive] in your knowledge of our Lord Jesus Christ. But [or for] anyone who does not have these things cannot see clearly [is nearsighted]. He is blind and [or because he] has forgotten that he was made clean from his past sins."
Galatians 5: 22-25; 2 Peter 1: 5-9. EXB

Chapter 13

WHOM SHALL I SEND?

*"Also I heard the voice of the Lord, saying: 'Whom shall I send? And who will go for us?' Then I said, '**Here am I! Send me**.' And He said, 'Go, and tell this people: "Keep on hearing, but do not understand; keep on seeing, but do not perceive." "For many are called, but few are chosen."*
Isaiah 6:8-9; Matthew 22:14. NKJV

There are a lot of people who desire to lead God's people, they are called to serve no doubt, but they are not chosen to lead God's people as senior pastors or overseers. They have the skills and experience to lead, but skill and experience don't call anyone to ministry leadership; God does. Real Christian leaders are born not human made, predestinated not human appointed. God told Jeremiah, before I formed you in your mother's womb I knew you, called and chose you. How do I know if God has chosen me? I cannot tell you, only God knows those whom He has chosen among the many He has called. He is your maker; He has your life's blueprint and decides your life purpose for you. Go to God in prayer and find out if you have been chosen. And if you have been chosen, ask Him what He chose you to do for Him and in Him.

"We know that in everything God works [or God works everything together; or everything works together] for the good of those who love him. They are the people he called, because that was his plan [according to his purpose]. God knew them before he made the world [For those whom he foreknew], and he chose them [he also predestined/chose beforehand] to be like [molded to the pattern of; conformed to <u>the image</u> of] his Son so that Jesus would be the firstborn [the preeminent one, but also indicating others will follow] of many brothers and sisters[Jesus' resurrection confirms that his followers will also share in God's glory]. And those God chose to be like his Son [predestined; chose

beforehand], he also called; and those he called, he also made right with him [declared righteous; justified]; and those he made right [declared righteous; justified], he also glorified [both a past act in Christ, and a future transformation].

The Lord spoke His word to me, saying: "Before I made [formed] you in your mother's womb, I chose [knew] you. Before you were born [came out of the womb], I set you apart for a special work [consecrated you]. I <u>appointed</u> you as a prophet to the nations." Then I said, "But Lord God, I don't know how to speak. I am only a boy [child; youth]." But the Lord said to me, "Don't say, 'I am only a boy [child; youth].' You must go everywhere I send you, and you must say everything I tell you to say [command you]. Don't be afraid of anyone, because I am with you to protect you," says the Lord. Then the Lord reached [sent] out his hand and touched my mouth [to consecrate it]. He said to me, "See, I am putting my words in your mouth. Today I have put you in charge of [appointed you over] nations and kingdoms. You will pull [pluck] up and tear [pull] down, destroy and overthrow, build up and plant [he will announce judgment and salvation]." Romans 8:28-30; Jeremiah 1: 4-10. EXB

Minister of God stop following the crowd

Many ministers of God are following the crowd not God, if the children of men make you, they can also break you. If men appointed you or make you a leader, they can also remove or fire you. But if God called and chose you, no human can fire you, because God is not a man. The devil is not foolish; he is the master of deception and confusion. He does not want you to fulfill God's purpose for your life. Satan will switch your destiny if you let him through people, or distract you from your original call of God, just to destroy you. He gives false, fake dreams, prophecies and visions.

The fact that you are a good speaker, a natural motivator or able to prophecy does not mean God has automatically chosen you to lead His people. If you make the mistake of following the crowd, because people tell you your head is fit for a crown based of your gifting, you may miss the mark. No matter how much people claim to love you, they will not stick with you if you fall, but if God called and chose you, He will without fail back you up. The gifts of God are given to us to serve, to benefit and to enrich the body of Christ, not to be used as a deceiving evidence of divine election. The Spirit of God gives gifts as He will to every believer in Christ, but divine election is only by predestination.

Many are called, but few are chosen

There is a big difference between when God Himself is our king, versus when we ask Him to give us a human king. Just as there is a big difference between when God chose you to lead as the head of a ministry or church, versus when God call you to serve under those whom He has chosen to lead as heads of ministries or churches. Don't forget, many are called to serve, but few among those that are called to serve are chosen to lead as heads. We cannot all be heads, nor can we all be servers. All fingers are not equal for a reason, yet they are all part of the same hand. So my beloved, find out if God called you to serve under those who are chosen to lead as heads, or you have been chosen to lead as the head? Remember, to whom much is given much will be expected.

"There are different kinds of gifts, but they are all from the same Spirit. There are different ways to serve [ministries] but the same Lord to serve. And there are different ways that God works through people [kinds of action; activities] but the same God works in all of us in everything we do [all things in all people]. Something from the Spirit can be seen in [The manifestation /disclosure of the Spirit is given to] each person, for the common good. The Spirit gives one person the ability to speak with wisdom [message/word of wisdom], and the same Spirit gives another the ability to speak with knowledge [message/word of knowledge]. The same Spirit gives faith to one person. And, to another, that one Spirit gives gifts of healing. The Spirit gives to

another person the <u>power</u> to do miracles [works of power], to another the ability to prophesy [prophecy]. And he gives to another the ability to know the difference between good and evil [discernment/distinguishing of] spirits.

The Spirit gives one person the ability to speak in different kinds of languages [or ecstatic utterance; tongues] and to another the ability to interpret those languages [interpretation of tongues]. One Spirit, the same Spirit, does all these things, and the Spirit decides what to give [distributes just as he wishes to] each person. And Christ gave gifts to people —he made some to be apostles, some to be prophets, some to go and tell the Good News, and some to have the work of caring for and teaching God's people [he himself gave apostles, prophets, evangelists, pastors/shepherds, and teachers]. Christ gave those gifts to <u>prepare</u> [to equip] God's holy people for the work of serving, to make the body of Christ stronger." 1 Corinthians 12:4-12; Ephesians 4: 11-12. EXB

Minster of God, please return to your original call

Many ministers of God have left their original call of God or divine election. It is not because they are following the crowd, but they have been distracted, thus greed, lust and pride has crept in on them on aware. They are still serving God, but not in the area or capacity God has ordained or chosen them to serve. A pastor turned himself into a prophet, a prophet now a pastor; an evangelist now an apostle, and an apostle now a prophet, while a teacher is now an apostle. Some are now frustrated and have since left serving God into playing con games to survive. Some church leaders were initially chosen by God, but have backslidden and are now false church leaders.

Some leaders were never chosen, they thought about how pastors and church leaders are becoming rich overnight and they call and chose themselves to ministry. Now they are using witchcraft and satanic means to sustain themselves through manipulation and con games. The devil has hired some church leaders to work for him or with him. We are in the last days; even the antichrist will do miracles and perform wonders. Don't be deceived. They will come to you in sheep's clothing, when in fact they are ravaging wolves. If you want to know more about how fake and manipulative, corrupt pastors and church leaders operate, please get our book titled, "Pastors' And Church Leaders' Con Games." If you have made a mistake and abandoned your original call of God as a leader to serve money, lust and materialism, it is not too late to return to your original call. Please go back to your original calling, return to your Bethel! Don't spend your whole life fulfilling the destiny God has not given you, only to get the greatest shock of your life on the day of reward.

"But I have this against you: You have left [abandoned] the love you had in the beginning [or your first love]. So remember [consider] where you were before you fell [how far you have fallen]. Change your hearts [Repent] and do what [the works] you did at first. If you do not change [repent], I will come to you and will take away your lamp-stand from its place." Genesis 35: 1; Revelation 2: 4-5. EXB

Chapter 14

How does God lead?

If God expect you and me to lead His way, we have to know how He Himself led, for us to be able to lead His way. God is not a joker, He is not partial or a task master who place heavy burden on the shoulders of others and sit around doing nothing, just dishing out orders. Our God is a good God, all His ways, works and wisdom are perfectly good all the time. It is good to note that God will never ask us to do what He cannot do Himself, He is a doer and yet a humble God. He is the almighty, the all powerful God, there is none greater than Him, yet He humbled Himself, came down to earth as a man to seek and save you and I that are byproducts of dust. His grace empower us to lead His people His way, when we learn how to be powerless in ourselves and how not to lean on our own understanding, but to rely on His unfailing love, amazing grace and faithfulness. God is daily seeking for leaders who will not only serve Him in spirit and in truth personally, but also those who can lead His people His way.

God lead by example

There is no greater and better leader than the Most High God Himself. He led by example. God want us to love, He knows love involves personal sacrifice for love to be real and complete either by nature or by design. God gave us His only begotten Son (Jesus Christ) to die for you and I as the proof of His exemplarily love. God commands us to love others, and He demonstrated it by loving us even when we cared less or have any atom of love for Him. Jesus dead for us while we were still sinners. God expect you and I to not just talk about His love but to always demonstrate His love in words and in deeds as He does.

"The Word became a human [flesh] and lived [made his home; pitched his tabernacle; God's glorious presence dwelt in Israel's tabernacle in the wilderness] among us. We saw his glory

[majesty]—the glory that belongs to the only Son [one and only; only begotten] of [who came from] the Father—and he was full of grace and truth [God's gracious love and faithfulness; But God shows [demonstrates; proves] his great [own] love for us in this way: Christ died for us while we were still sinners. We love because God [He] first loved us."
John 1: 14; Romans 5: 8; 1 John 4: 19. EXB

God in Christ came to serve us

God in Christ and through Christ came to earth not only to save us, but also to serve us. There is no doubt that when Jesus who is both God and man demonstrated selfless humility by being born in a merger, he was teaching us the path to servant leadership. Jesus Himself did not hide His passion to love, to serve and to save us. Jesus expects us to serve His flocks in humility.

"For even the Son of Man came not to be served but to serve others and to give his life as a ransom for many."
Matthew 20:28. NLT

God is the shepherd of our lives

There is no better shepherd we can ask for other than God Himself, who is good, loves and cares for us unconditionally. God expect us to be good shepherds to His flocks and to lead them His way not ours. King David said, the Lord is my shepherd, I shall not want. Some of the leaders God called to shepherd His flocks has failed Him by preying on His people. God does not want you to fail Him or prey on His people as a leader, rather He want you to lead His flocks His way. I am believing God, that you will be that good shepherd after God's heart like King David. God did not choose David the shepherd boy because of his power or might, David was chosen because he had a heart after God—he had a shepherd's heart.

"And I will give you [spiritual] shepherds after My own heart [in the final time], who will feed you with knowledge and understanding and judgment." Jeremiah 3:15.

"After God took him away [removed/deposed him], God made David [raised up David as] their king. God said [witnessed; testified] about him: 'I have found in David son of Jesse the kind of man I want [man whose heart is like mine; a man after my own heart]. He will do [or accomplish] all I want him to do [my will]. Be careful for [Keep watch over] yourselves and for all the people [flock] the Holy Spirit has given to you to oversee [made you overseers/guardians]. You must be like shepherds to the church of God, which he bought [or obtained] with the death of his own Son [with the blood of his own (Son); or with his own blood]." Acts 13: 22; 20: 28. EXB

God lead us by delegation

God sent Jesus into the world for our sakes, and Jesus has sent us into the world for the sake of our fellow men.

"And He who sent Me is with Me. The Father has not left Me alone, for I always do those things that please Him. So Jesus said to them again, peace to you! As the Father has sent Me, I also send you." John 8: 29; 20: 21. NKJV

God empower us to lead

God is the greatest example of delegation and leadership empowerment. God the Father delegated the task of saving mankind to Jesus, and empowered Him with all the powers He needed to complete the task. Jesus also has delegated the great commission to us and has empowered us with His Spirit, Name, Blood and Word to help us succeed. If you as a leader seek to lead God's way, you must not only delegate, you must also empower those you delegate and give them freedom to act just has Jesus Christ did for you.

"The Father loves the Son and has given him power over everything [him authority over all; all things into his hand]. Then Jesus came to them and said, "All power [authority] in heaven and on earth is [has been] given to me." Listen [Look; Behold], I have given you power [authority] to walk on [trample] snakes and

scorpions, power that is greater than the enemy has [and authority over all the power of the enemy]. So nothing will hurt you."
John 3: 35; Matthew 28: 18; Luke 10: 19. EXB

God is committed to our success in ministry

God is greatly committed to our success; His thoughts toward us are not of evil but of good, to give us a hope and a future. The reason why you and I are still serving God is because He is holy, faithful and true. God expect you too to be holy, faithful and true; trustworthy and courageous no matter the odds combating your soul as you carry out His life saving mission here on earth. Jesus suffered on the Cross because of you and I. God has promised to never forsake you when you are going through life's problems. He said I will be with you. Kind David said, "even though I walk through the valley of the shadow of death, I will fear no evil because God is with me." Take care of God's flocks, don't abandon then in their time of weakness, when they fall, or when they are going through their own valley of the shadow of death.

"Now this is what the Lord says. He created you, people of Jacob [Jacob]; He formed you, people of Israel [Israel].He says, "Don't be afraid, because I have saved [ransomed; redeemed] you. I have called you by name, and you are mine. When you pass through the waters, I will be with you [as at the Red/or Reed Sea]. When you cross rivers, you will not drown [they will not overflow you; as when Israel crossed the Jordan River into the Promised Land]. When you walk through fire, you will not be burned, nor will the flames hurt you." Isaiah 43: 1-2. EXB

God lead us with patience, teaching us how to live

There is no leader in the world that is as patient, loving, merciful, and forgiving as our God. No one of us is worthy of His great love, yet while we were yet sinners, Jesus died for us. God forgives us our sins, and heal our wounds, any time we humble ourselves before His throne of grace and mercy. For it is by His mercy and compassion that we are not consumed when we disobey Him, and play the games of pretense with Him. We commit or fall into sin from time to time, but His great love covers the multitudes of our sins; and His mercy often prevail over His judgment; which is why we are consumed by His consuming fire nature. Sometimes we give the glory due His holy name to graven images, Satan and ourselves (our pride, arrogance and exaggeration), yet the shed blood of His Son Jesus Christ avails and atone for us each time. God want you and I to be forgivers, just as He forgives us. If we refuse to forgive our offenders, we are telling God to put the forgiveness of our own sins on hold, until we are ready to forgive and let go, so we can let Him have His way in our lives.

"My whole being [O my soul], praise [bless] the Lord and do not forget all his kindnesses [gifts; benefits]. He forgives all my [or your] sins [iniquity] and heals all my [or your] diseases [ills]. He saves [redeems] my [or your] life from the grave [pit] and loads [or crowns] me [or you] with love [loyalty] and mercy [compassion]. He satisfies me [or you] with good things [as long as you live; or according to your desires] and makes me young again [renews your youth], like the eagle. The Lord does what is right [righteous] and fair [just] for all who are wronged by others [oppressed; exploited].

He showed [revealed] his ways to Moses and his deeds to the people [sons] of Israel. The Lord shows mercy [compassion] and is kind [grace]. He does not become angry quickly [is slow to anger], and he has great love [loyalty]. He will not always accuse [charge; contend with] us, and he will not be angry forever [keep watch forever]. He has not punished us as our sins should be punished [does not act toward us according to our sins]; he has not repaid us for the evil we have done [according to our iniquity]. As high as the sky [heaven] is above the earth, so great is his love [loyalty] for those who respect [fear] him. He has taken our sins [transgressions] away from us as far as the east is from west. The Lord has mercy [compassion] on those who respect [fear] him, as a father has mercy [compassion] on his children. He knows how we were made [formed]; he remembers that we are dust." Psalm 103: 2-14. EXB

God expect you as His chosen leader to lead His way

There are biblical instructions you and I must always follow as we lead God's people. We must be careful not to deviate from God's way, plan and purpose. God warned Moses the man of God to be very careful to build the tabernacle as He has instructed and that Moses must not deviate from the laid down plan or way. Jesus Christ is the one and only true foundation of Christianity. You and I must build God's church on no other foundation, except on Jesus Christ our firm foundation.

"Be very careful to make them by the plan [pattern] I showed you on the mountain." Exodus 25: 40. EXB

"In all the work you are doing, work the best you can [do it heart and soul; from the soul]. Work as if you were doing it for the Lord, not for people. Remember [knowing] that you will receive from the Lord the reward which he promised to his people [of an inheritance]. You are serving the Lord Christ." Colossian 3: 23-24.

I encourage you to always do what Jesus would do as you lead God's people. As you care for God's flocks, always ask yourself this question, ***"How would Jesus handle this or what would Jesus do in this kind of situation?"*** We can deceive men, we cannot deceive God, He cannot be mocked, whatever you and I sow, we will also reap. If you are lead God's people His way and or your ways, God is the judge, He will reward you accordingly. Always remember that what you do to any one of God's flock you are doing to God Himself.

"When the Son of Man comes in his glory, and all the angels with him, he will sit on his glorious throne. All the nations will be gathered before him, and he will separate the people one from another as a shepherd separates the sheep from the goats. He will put the sheep on his right and the goats on his left. "Then the King

will say to those on his right, 'Come, you who are blessed by my Father; take your inheritance, the kingdom prepared for you since the creation of the world. For I was hungry and you gave me something to eat, I was thirsty and you gave me something to drink, I was a stranger and you invited me in, I needed clothes and you clothed me, I was sick and you looked after me, I was in prison and you came to visit me.' "Then the righteous will answer him, 'Lord, when did we see you hungry and feed you, or thirsty and give you something to drink? When did we see you a stranger and invite you in, or needing clothes and clothe you? When did we see you sick or in prison and go to visit you?' The King will reply, 'Truly I tell you, whatever you did for one of the least of these brothers and sisters of mine, you did for me.'"
Matthew 25: 31-40. NIV

Bear fruits that will not parish

"But the fruit of the [Holy] Spirit [the work which His presence within accomplishes] is love, joy (gladness), peace, patience (an even temper, forbearance), kindness, goodness (benevolence), faithfulness, Gentleness (meekness, humility), self-control (self-restraint, continence). Against such things there is no law [that can bring a charge]." Galatians 5: 22-23.

Chapter 15

God want quality not quantity

There is no big or small ministry as far as servitude is concerned, because we all have and enjoy diversity of gifts by the same Spirit. It is sad to note that some leaders called themselves into ministry. Some were called into ministry by fellow men. God does not measure our relationship with Him or our success in the ministry by quantity, ministry size, earthly possessions or titles. He is a God of order. God want quality, not quantity. We serve a quality God, who is excellent in power, glorious in holiness and fearful in praises. Don't get carried away by numbers, earthly goods or fame, because a man's life does not consist of the abundance of things he possesses. Give God your best in your obedience, worship and service life. Love Him with all your heart without compromise and do all can to live your daily life for His glory. God created you and I for His glory. Stop playing church, the Lord's work must be done the Lord's way or no other.

A true leader must be crucified with Christ

"So I am not the one living now—it is Christ living in me. I still live in my body, but I live by faith in the Son of God. He is the one who loved me and gave himself to save me."
Galatians 2:20. ERV

A leader who has been crucified with Christ must be dead to self and must be willing to give up personal experience, all human invented doctrines or traditional methods of leadership, and personal interests and lead God's people God's way based on biblical standards. Don't forget you are ever a child in His eyes regardless of all the human fame, accolades or titles you may have acquired here on earth. The powers of darkness does not respect or honor titles, they will only bow to the name of Jesus and without fail respect and honor the anointing of the living God on your life.

Christian leader take heed

Dear Christian leader, take heed. I encourage you to lead God's people God's way, not your way. They are God's flocks, not your toys. God will without fail hold you accountable for His flocks. If you are already leading God's people God's way that is good, your labor of love, sacrifice and tears will not be in vain. Keep your eyes ever on Jesus Christ, the author and finisher of our faith. It is my sincere prayer that you will finish well and strong, and be able to say at the end like the apostle Paul with hope and confidence, "I have finished the course, I have ran well and fought the good fight of faith, now is laid up for me the crown of glory."

"The Lord says, "I will make you wise [instruct you] and show [teach] you where to [the way you should] go. I will guide [counsel] you and watch over [my eye will be on] you. Be careful for [Keep watch over] yourselves and for all the people [flocks] the Holy Spirit has given to you to oversee [made you overseers /guardians]. You must be like shepherds to the church of God, which he bought [or obtained] with the death of his own Son [with the blood of his own (Son); or with his own blood]."
Psalm 32:8; Acts 20:28. EXB

Who are the greatest ministers of God?

The greatest ministers of God are not those who lead big or mega churches or ministries, nor are they those who are the richest or most famous among ministers. They are those who minister to the Lord, and lead God's people God's way. Ministering to God is our first ministry. When you minister to God, He will fill you with His Spirit, power and grace to minister to His people. Don't minister to the children of men until you have first minister to God. When God is the one ministering through you, lives will be transformed, sinners will be saved and backsliders will be restored. When you don't minister to God first, His presence will not be available to save and to heal, so you will minister in the flesh. The flesh does no good, the letter kills. It is the Spirit that gives life.

"Seek first [Be concerned above all else with] God's kingdom and what God wants [his righteousness]. Then all your other needs will be met as well [these things will be given to you]. "Then the Lord appeared to Solomon at night and said to him, "I have heard your prayer and have chosen this place for myself to be a Temple [house] for [of] sacrifices. "I may [If] stop the sky [shut the heavens] from sending rain. I may [or if I] command the locusts to destroy [devour] the land. I may [or if I] send sicknesses [plague; pestilence] to my people. Then if my people, who are called by my name [belong to me], will humble themselves, if they will pray and seek me [my face] and stop their evil ways, I will hear them from heaven. I will forgive their sin, and I will heal [restore] their land. Now I will see them, and I will listen [my eyes will be open and my ears attentive] to the prayers prayed in this place. I have chosen this Temple [house] and made it holy [consecrate /purified/sanctified it]. So I will be worshiped [my name will be] there forever. Yes, I will always watch over it and love it [my eyes and my heart will be there forever]."* Matthew 6: 33; 2 Chronicles 7:12-16. EXB

Rely on God not on the gift He gave you

Many Christian leaders called by God have turned their backs on God and fallen from the faith even though they are still in key positions or still celebrated eloquent preachers, but they are now mere entertainers and motivational speakers. Nice talkers they are, their words are void of the saving power of the Holy Spirit, and their preaching or teachings are often mingled with flesh and relevant human traditions and views. So many church leaders have fallen from the faith, and are living on past glories. So many leaders have lost their vision of faith because their eyes are no more fixed on Jesus, but on worldly riches and wealth.

Jesus is coming either to judge or reward us

"The Son of Man will come again with divine greatness, and all His angels will come with Him. He will sit as king on his great and glorious throne. All the people of the world will be gathered before Him. Then he will separate everyone into two groups. It will

be like a shepherd separating his sheep from his goats. He will put the sheep on His right and the goats on His left. "Then the king will say to the godly people on His right, 'Come, my Father has great blessings for you. The kingdom He promised is now yours. It has been prepared for you since the world was made. It is yours because when I was hungry, you gave me food to eat. When I was thirsty, you gave me something to drink. When I had no place to stay, you welcomed me into your home. When I was without clothes, you gave me something to wear. When I was sick, you cared for me. When I was in prison, you came to visit me.' 'Then the godly people will answer, 'Lord, when did we see you hungry and give you food? When did we see you thirsty and give you something to drink? When did we see you with no place to stay and welcome you into our home? When did we see you without clothes and give you something to wear? When did we see you sick or in prison and care for you?'

"Then the king will answer, 'the truth is, anything you did for any of my people here, you also did for me.' "Then the king will say to the evil people on his left, 'Get away from me. God has already decided that you will be punished. Go into the fire that burns forever—the fire that was prepared for the devil and his angels. You must go away because when I was hungry, you gave me nothing to eat. When I was thirsty, you gave me nothing to drink. When I had no place to stay, you did not welcome me into your home. When I was without clothes, you gave me nothing to wear. When I was sick and in prison, you did not care for me.' "Then those people will answer, 'Lord, when did we see you hungry or thirsty? When did we see you without a place to stay? Or when did we see you without clothes or sick or in prison? When did we see any of this and not help you?'

"The king will answer, 'the truth is, anything you refused to do for any of my people here, you refused to do for me.' "Then these evil people will go away to be punished forever. But the godly people will go and enjoy eternal life."
Matthew 25:31-46. ERV

Lead God's people God's way

Again, I tell you the truth, that it is possible to raise the dead, heal the sick, cast out demons, be financially free here on earth and at the end go to hell. God require obedience not sacrifices. Many of us leaders have good intentions for trying to bend the rules, we often forget that we cannot help or mock God. Obedience to God is the proof of our love for Him; you can manipulate, trick and deceive man, not God. He want you and me to lead His people— His way, not our own way, or any other way. As far as God is concerned, it is His way or no other. Jesus Christ is the one and only true way to God. Jesus Christ is our perfect example He came to show you and I how to lead God's people God's way, even though He Himself was the way. I encourage you in the name of the Lord, lead God's people God's way not your way. Please form the habit of auditing your life, your relationship with God and how you are leading His people, so you don't win the world and end up a castaway.

"On the last day [judgment day; that day] many people will say to me, 'Lord, Lord, we spoke for you [Did we not prophesy in your name?], and through you we forced out demons [cast out demons in your name?] and did many miracles [mighty works in your name?].' Then I will tell them clearly [declare to them; publicly announce to them], 'I never knew you. Get away [Depart] from me, you who do evil [break God's law; practice lawlessness].' Everyone who hears my words and obeys [acts on; practices] them, is like a wise [sensible] man who built his house on rock. It rained hard, the floods came [rivers rose], and the winds blew and hit [beat; slammed against] that house. But it did not fall [collapse], because it was built on rock. Everyone who hears my words and does not obey [act on; practice] them, is like a foolish [stupid] man who built his house on sand. It rained hard, the floods came [rivers rose], and the winds blew and hit [beat; slammed against] that house, and it fell [collapsed] with a big crash." Matthew 7:22-27. EXB

Finally, put on the whole armor of God

The fact that you have been called and chosen by God does not mean that you will not face life's troubles and challenges. The devil will try to do everything he can to stop you, steal your joy, kill your relationship with God or destroy your determination and passion to lead God's people God's way. Never take the devil for granted, sin is his greatest weapon and holiness is your greatest defense. I encourage you my beloved in the Lord, put on the whole armor of God every time, 24/7, never leave home, do anything or go anywhere without them because the days are evil.

"Finally, be strong in the Lord and in His great [strong; mighty] power. Put on the full armor of God so that you can fight against the devil's evil tricks [schemes]. [For] Our fight [conflict; struggle] is not against people on earth [flesh and blood] but against the rulers and authorities and the powers [or cosmic powers/rulers] of this world's darkness [darkness], against the spiritual powers of evil in the heavenly ·world [realm; places]. That is why you need to [For this reason,] put on God's full armor. Then on the day of evil [persecution generally or end-time tribulation] you will be able to stand strong [keep your ground; resist the enemy]. And when you have finished the whole fight [after you have done/accomplished everything], you will still be standing.

So stand strong [or ready], with the belt of truth tied around your waist and the body armor [breastplate] of right living [a righteous life; or God's own righteousness/justice; righteousness]. On your feet wear the Good News [Gospel] of peace to help you stand strong [for firm footing; or to be fully prepared]. And also [in addition to all this; or in all circumstances] use the shield of faith with which you can stop [extinguish] all the burning arrows [fiery darts] of the Evil One. Accept [Receive; or Take] the helmet of salvation, and take the sword of the Spirit, which is the word [message] of God. Pray in [or in dependence on] the Spirit at all times with all ·kinds of prayers [prayers and requests], asking for everything you need. To do this you must always be ready [alert] ·and never give up [with all perseverance]. Always pray for all God's people [the saints]." Ephesians 6:10-19. EXB

About the author

Joseph Blessing Omosigho has authored many life changing books and Spirit filled gospel songs. He is a pastor to pastors and a special gift from God to the body of Christ, church leaders and the world. To order books, or to book Pastor Joseph to come and minister, please give us a call, write or email today us at the address below.

Ministry of Christ
2013 Wellington Point,
Heartland, TX 75126
Tel: 214-994-8080
Online: winnerslane.org.
Email: ministryofchrist@gmail.com

May God bless you richly and perfect all that concerns you, in Jesus' name. Please, minister of God, church leader or head of department (deacon or deaconess), I beg you in the name of the LORD, GOD Almighty! Do all you can to lead God's people God's way while leaning on the everlasting arm of God that never fails. Can you lead God's way? Yes you can, His grace is sufficient for you, and you can do all things through Jesus Christ who strengthens you. I love you, but God loves you more!

"Therefore take heed to yourselves and to all the flock, among which the Holy Spirit has made you overseers, to shepherd the church of God which He purchased with His own blood. Finally, brethren, farewell (rejoice)! Be strengthened (perfected, completed, made what you ought to be); be encouraged and consoled and comforted; be of the same [agreeable] mind one with another; live in peace, and [then] the God of love [Who is the Source of affection, goodwill, love, and benevolence toward men] and the Author and Promoter of peace will be with you."
Acts 20:28; 2 Corinthians 13:11

www.ingramcontent.com/pod-product-compliance
Lightning Source LLC
Chambersburg PA
CBHW030109070426
42448CB00036B/590